I0471522

Ignoble Deaths
Tyler Landry

copyright 2022, Tyler Landry
978-1-387-88453-7

Leading up to, and during, the various covid19 pandemic lockdown/isolation periods, I started spending more time watching friends and internet acquaintances play and stream video games. It started out as accompaniment to drawing i was already doing, but eventually, i also started drawing what i was watching. This little booklet contains scenes from, or inspired by the games, and the people streaming them. Most of them are raw sketchbook fodder, while a handful manifested as digital painting or pixel art.

At the suggestion of a friend, i've compiled a bunch of those drawings and paintings here, as a little time capsule collection of media and headspace from those strange, dark times, which continue to mutate and challenge our collective lives.

An attempt to capture all of the extended community of streamers and viewers involved, and also spell their handles correctly, is a fool's errand, so I won't even try. That said, you know who you are. If you've seen ol' clavcity hangin' round your chat, pretending to be interesting and clever, trying to interact with you and your friends while playing games - thank you. Thanks for tolerating me, and for being cool and fun and hangout-worthy. This modest publication is dedicated to you.

Also, thanks Jon for unintentionally providing the title for this one.

TL, June 2022

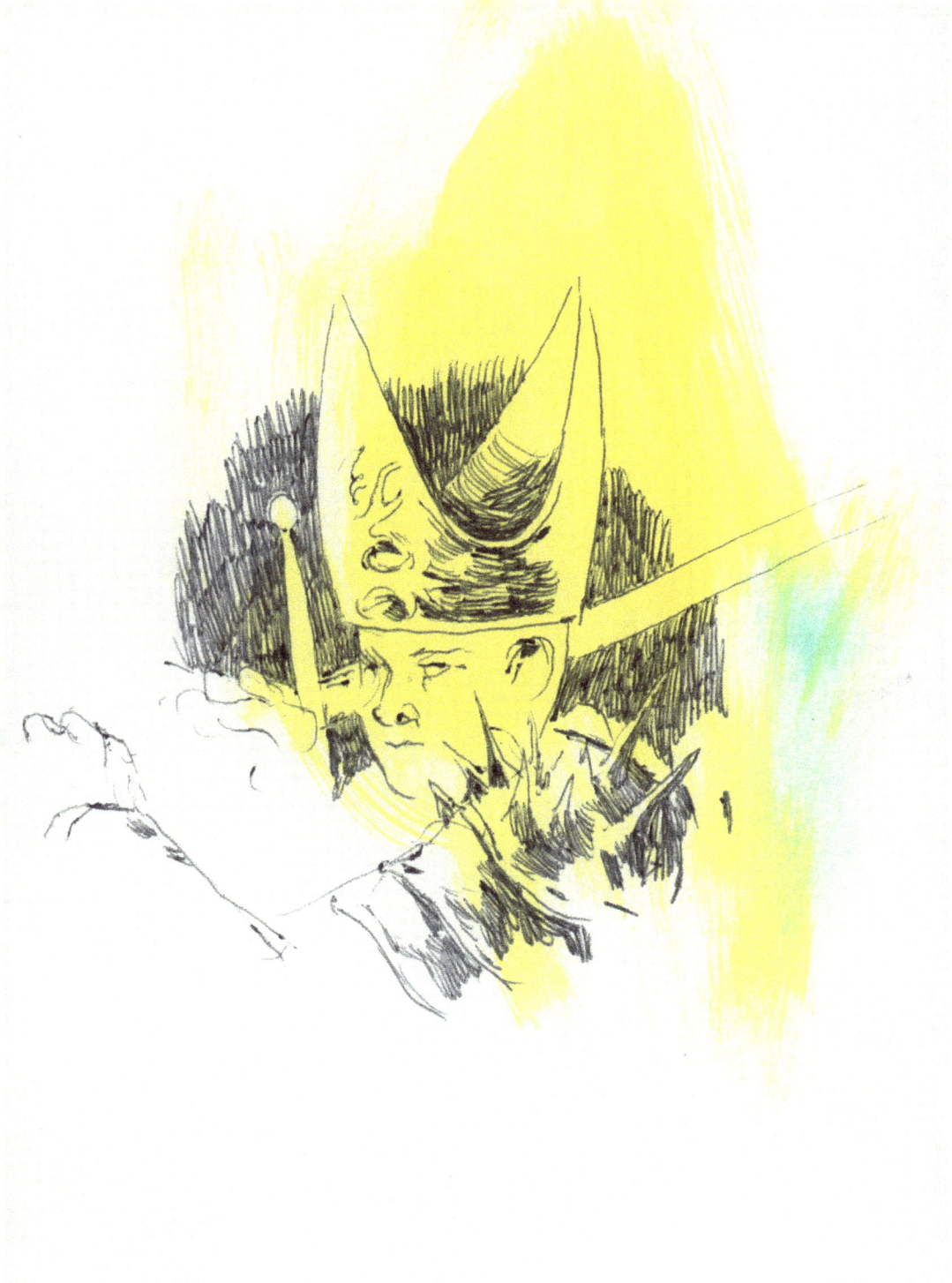

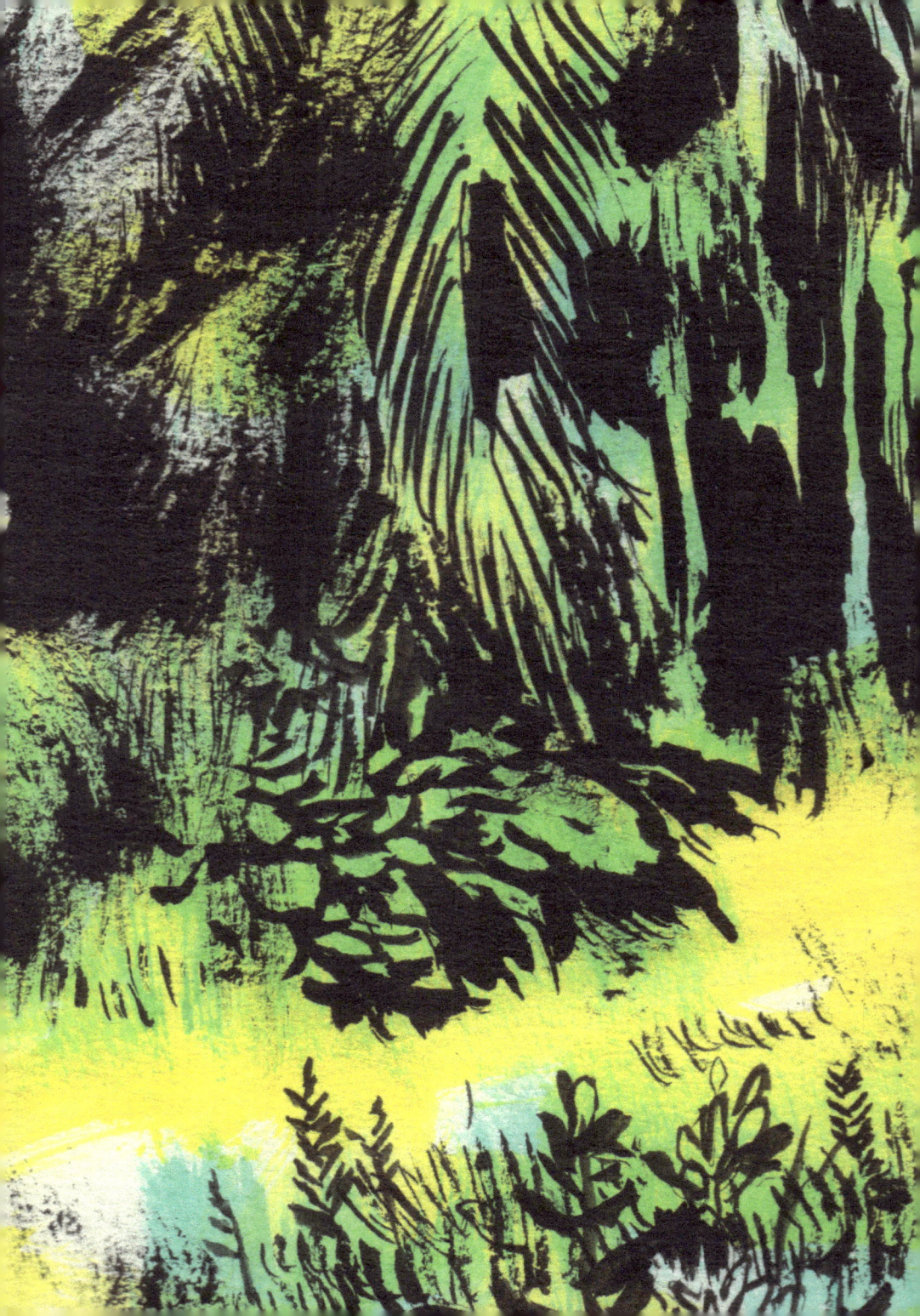

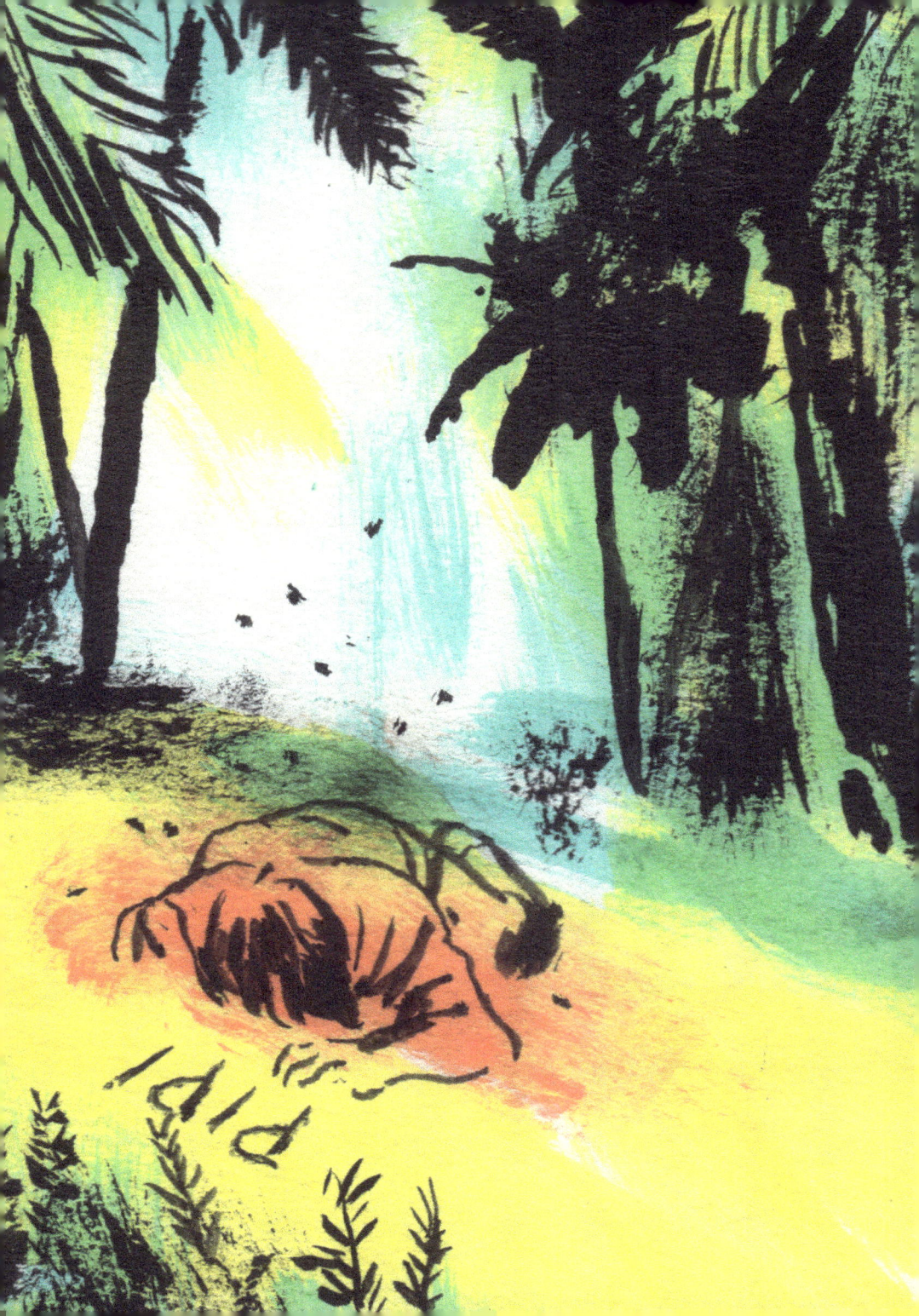

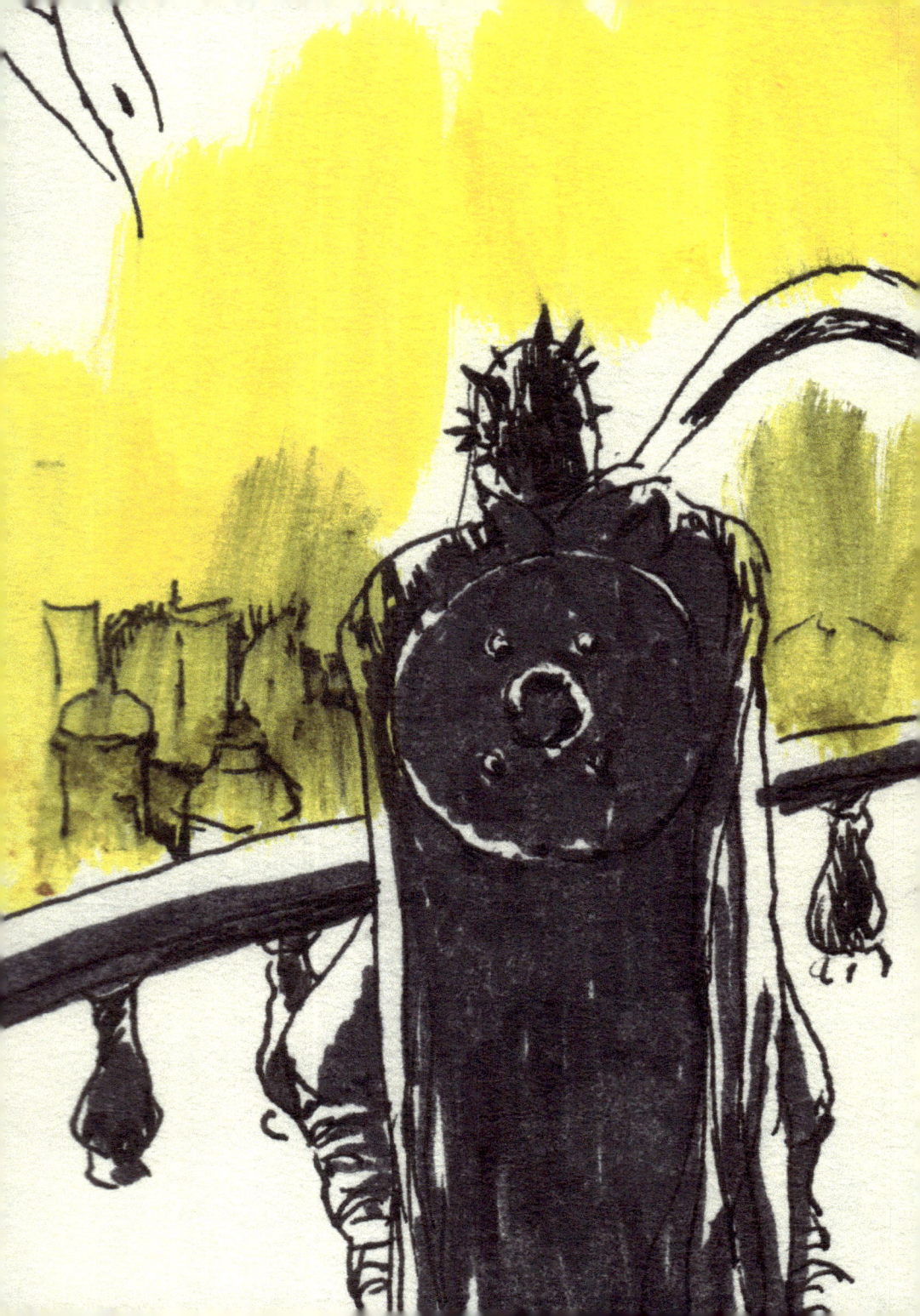

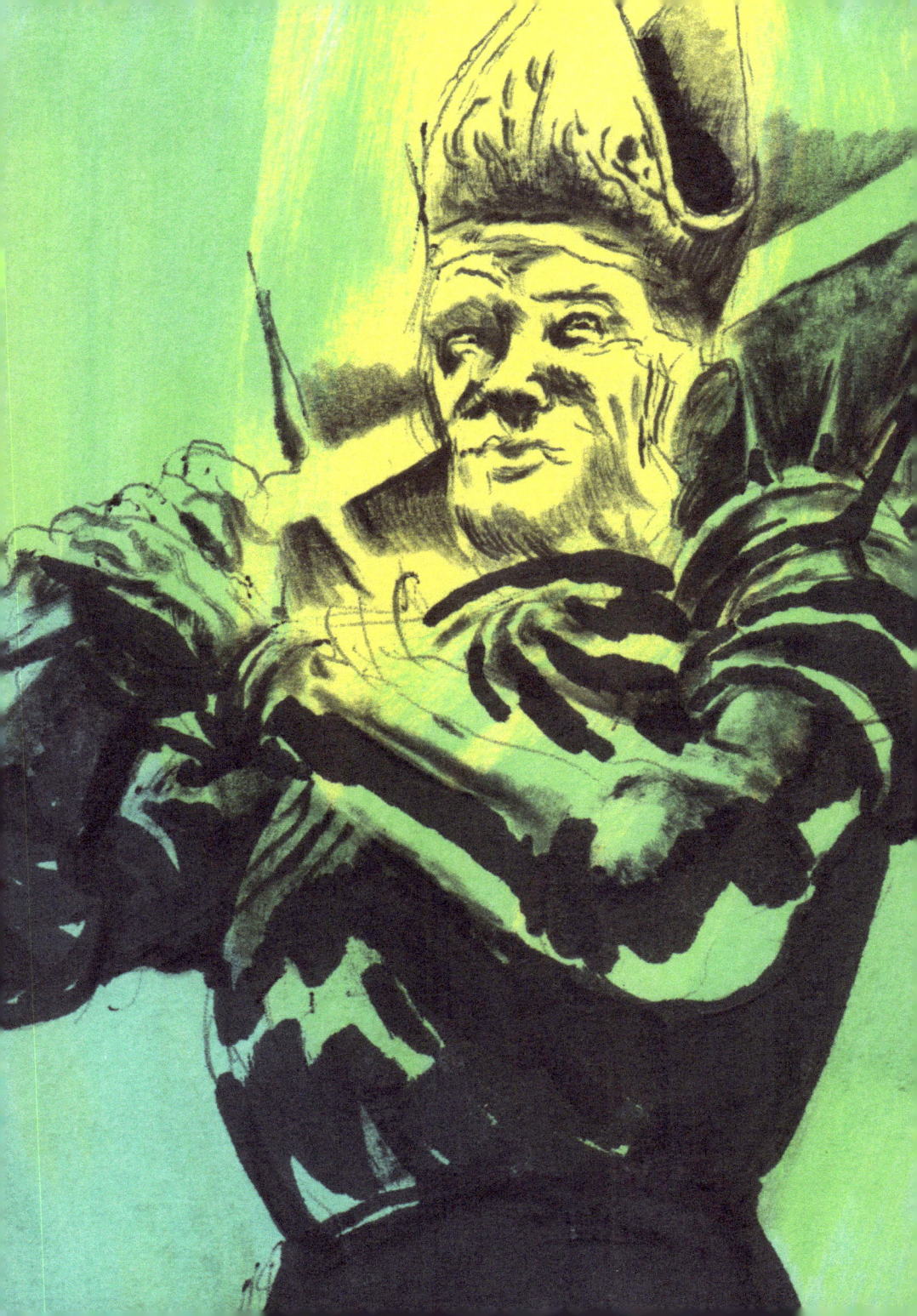

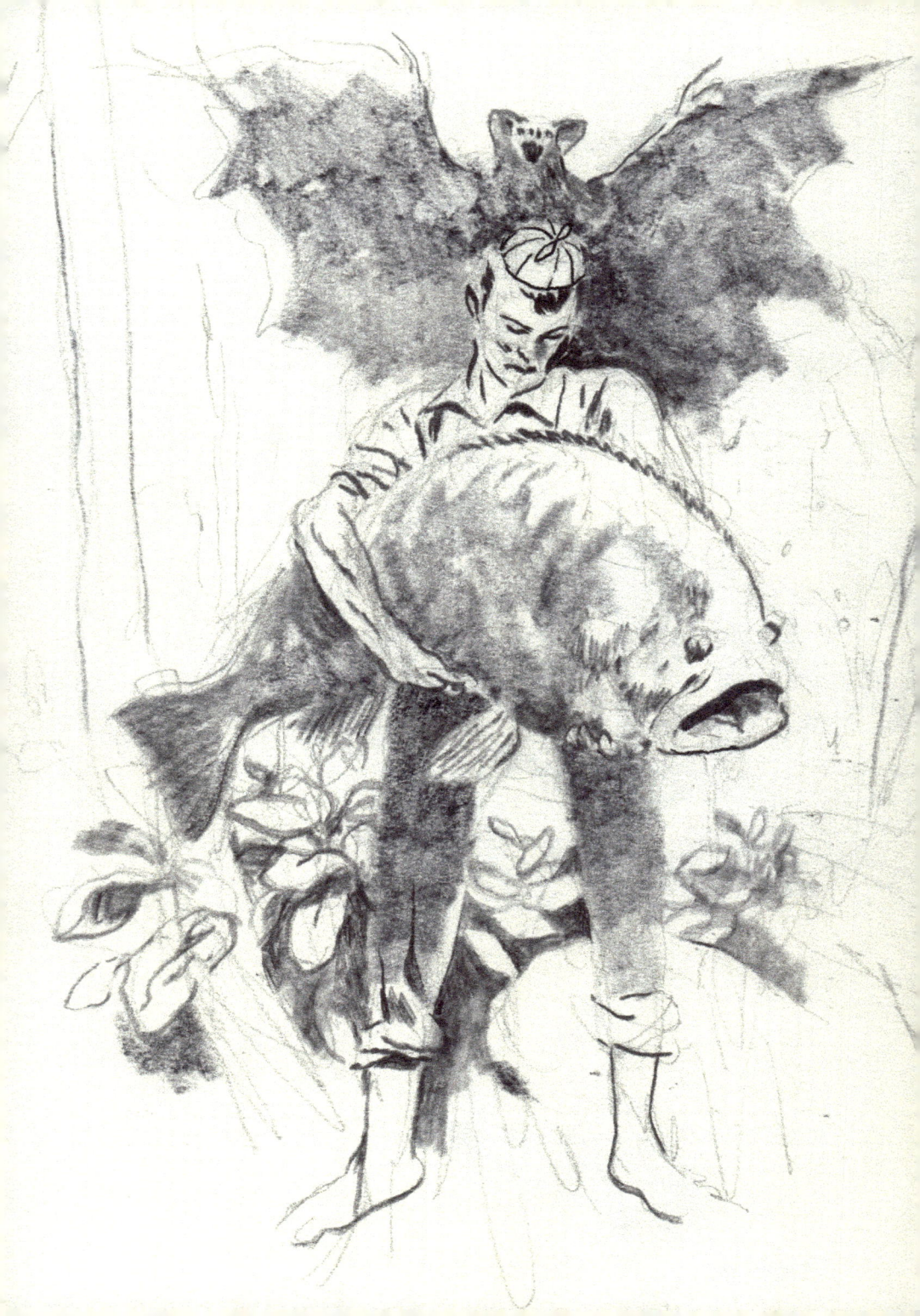

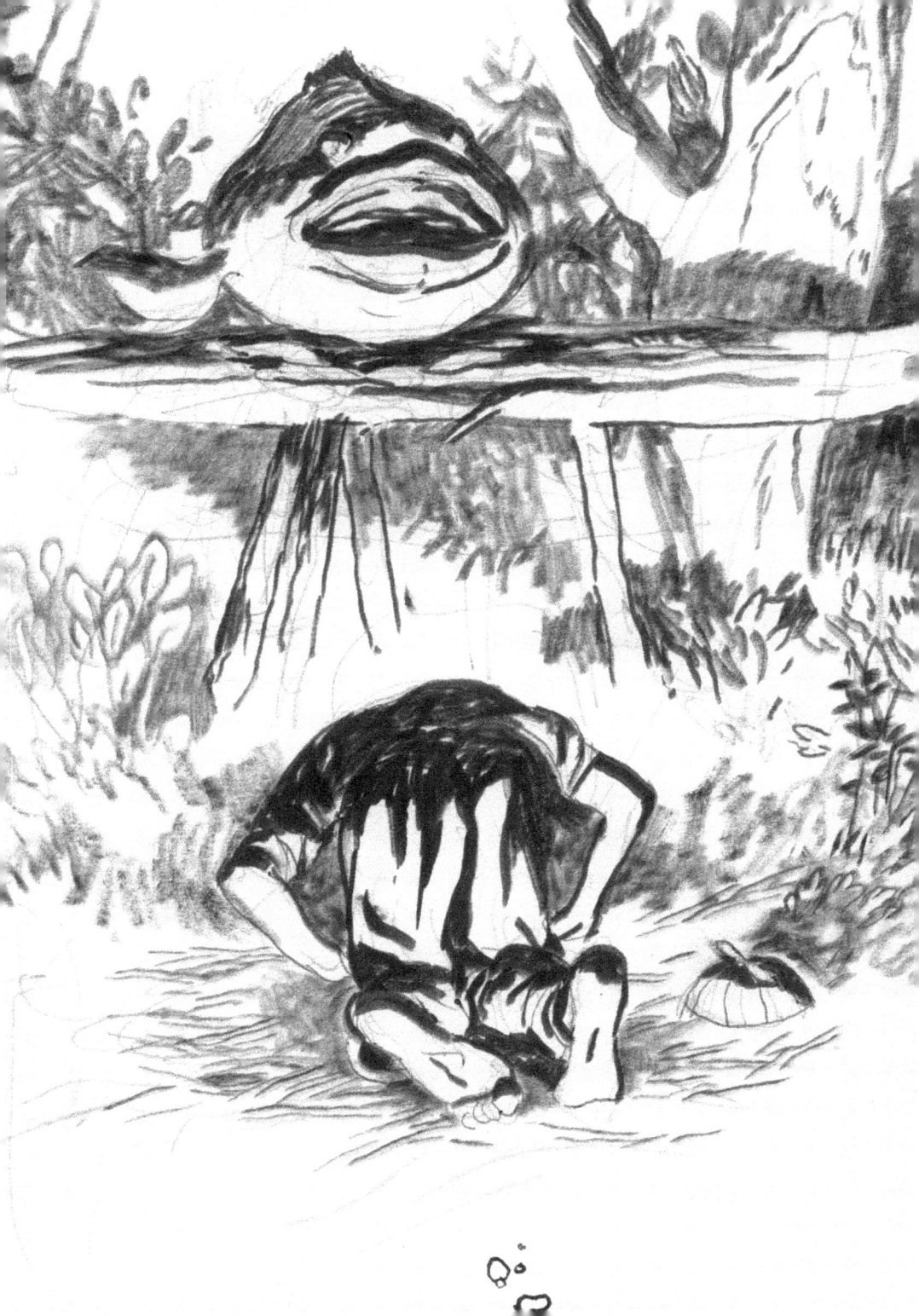

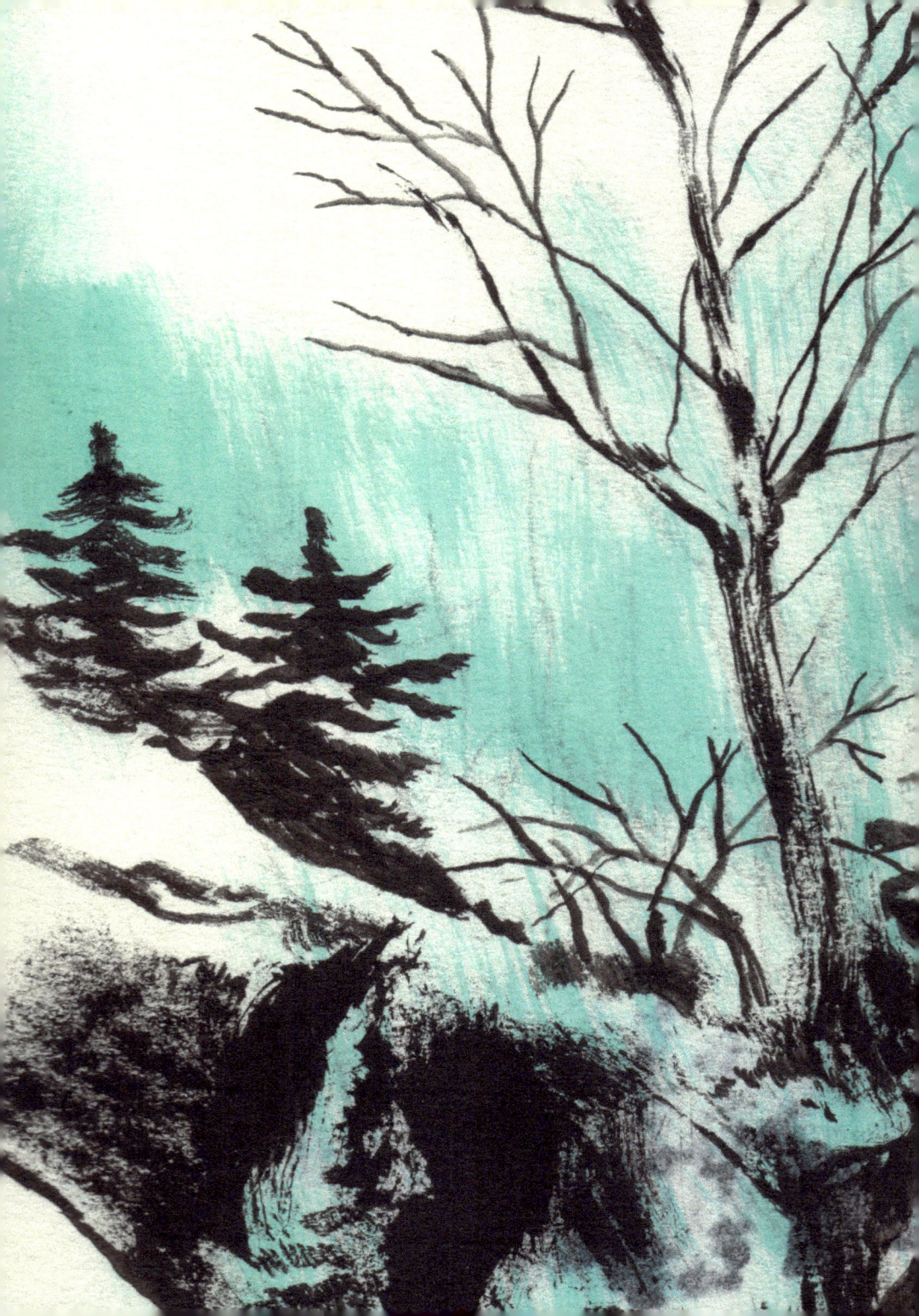

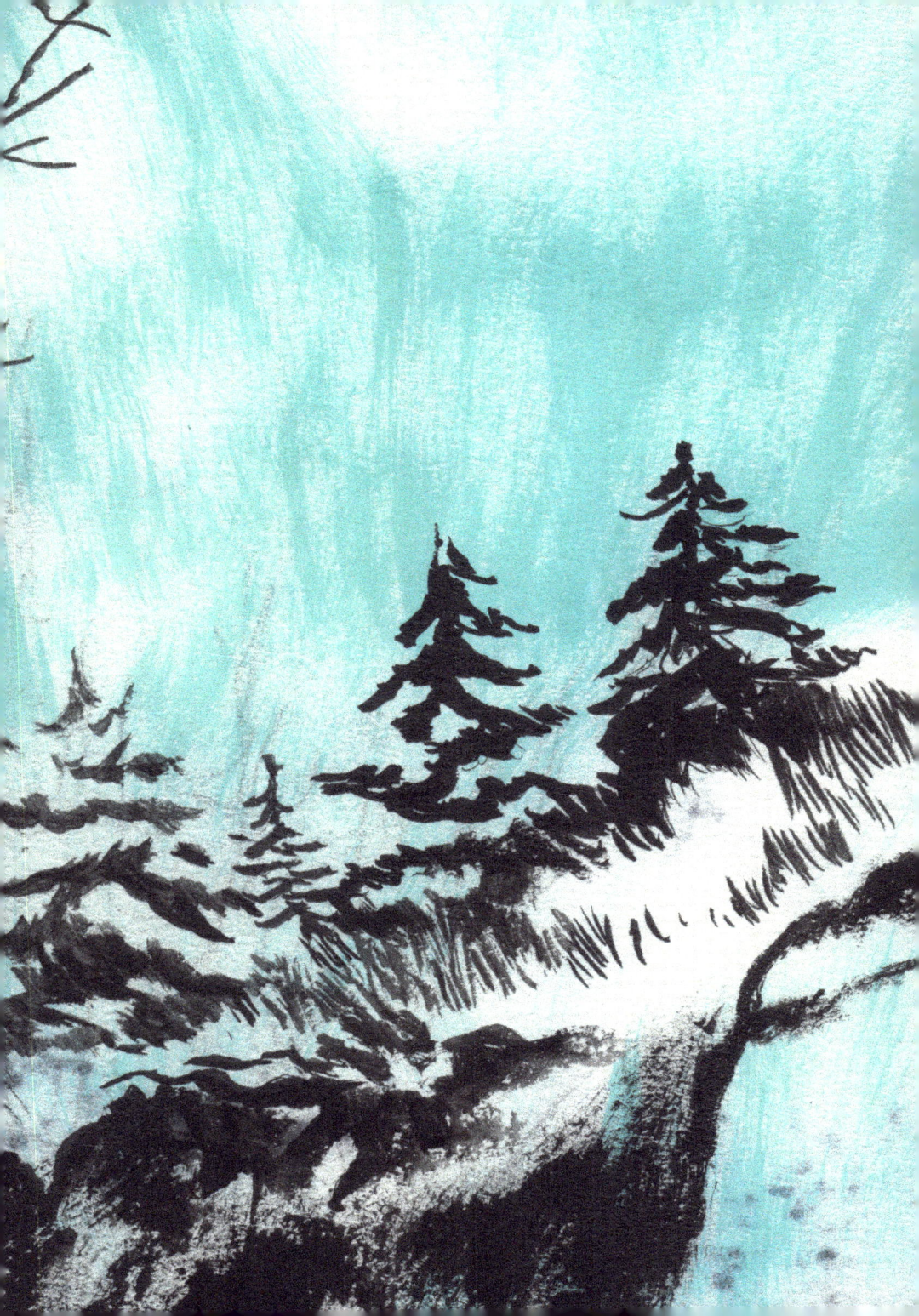

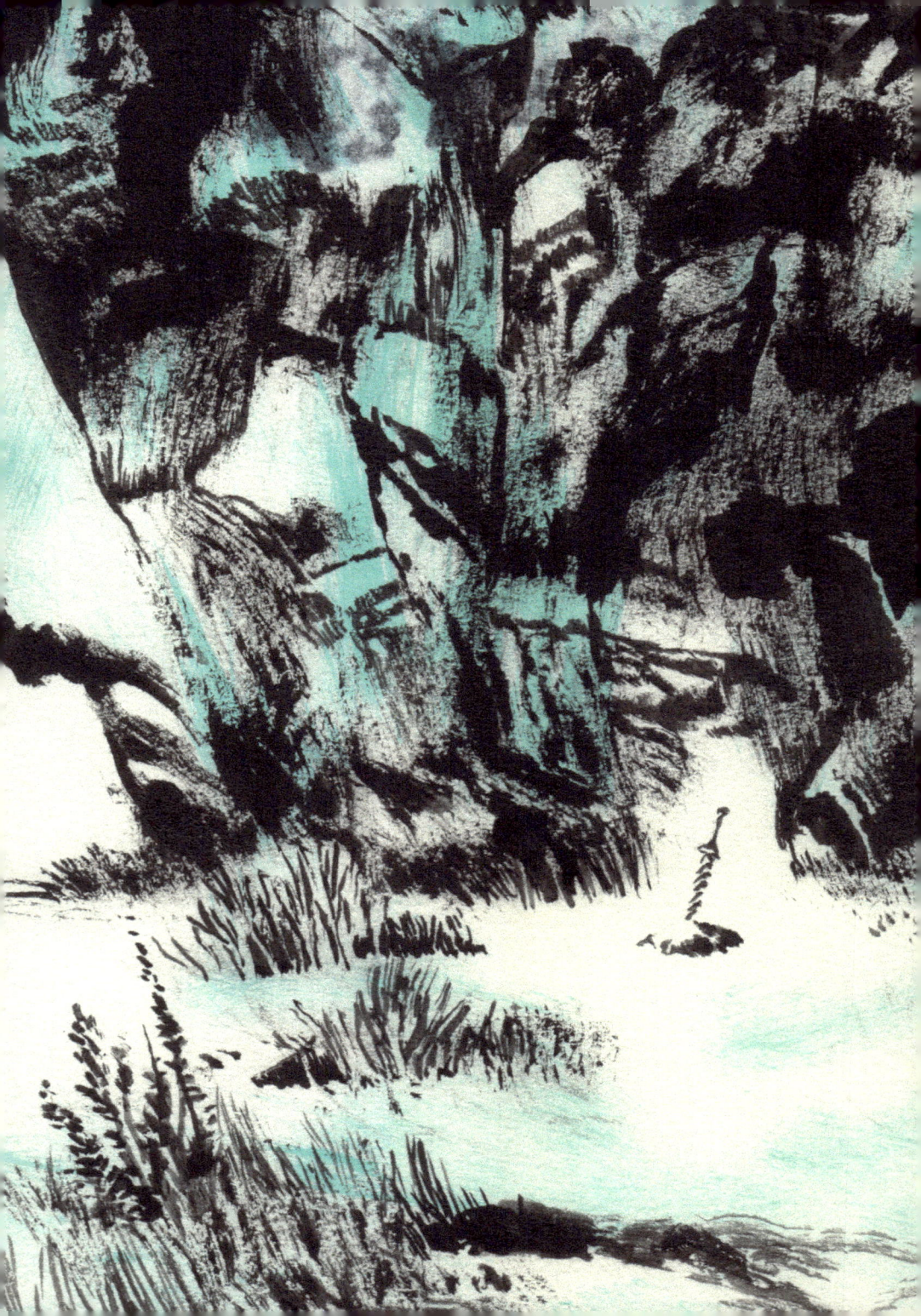

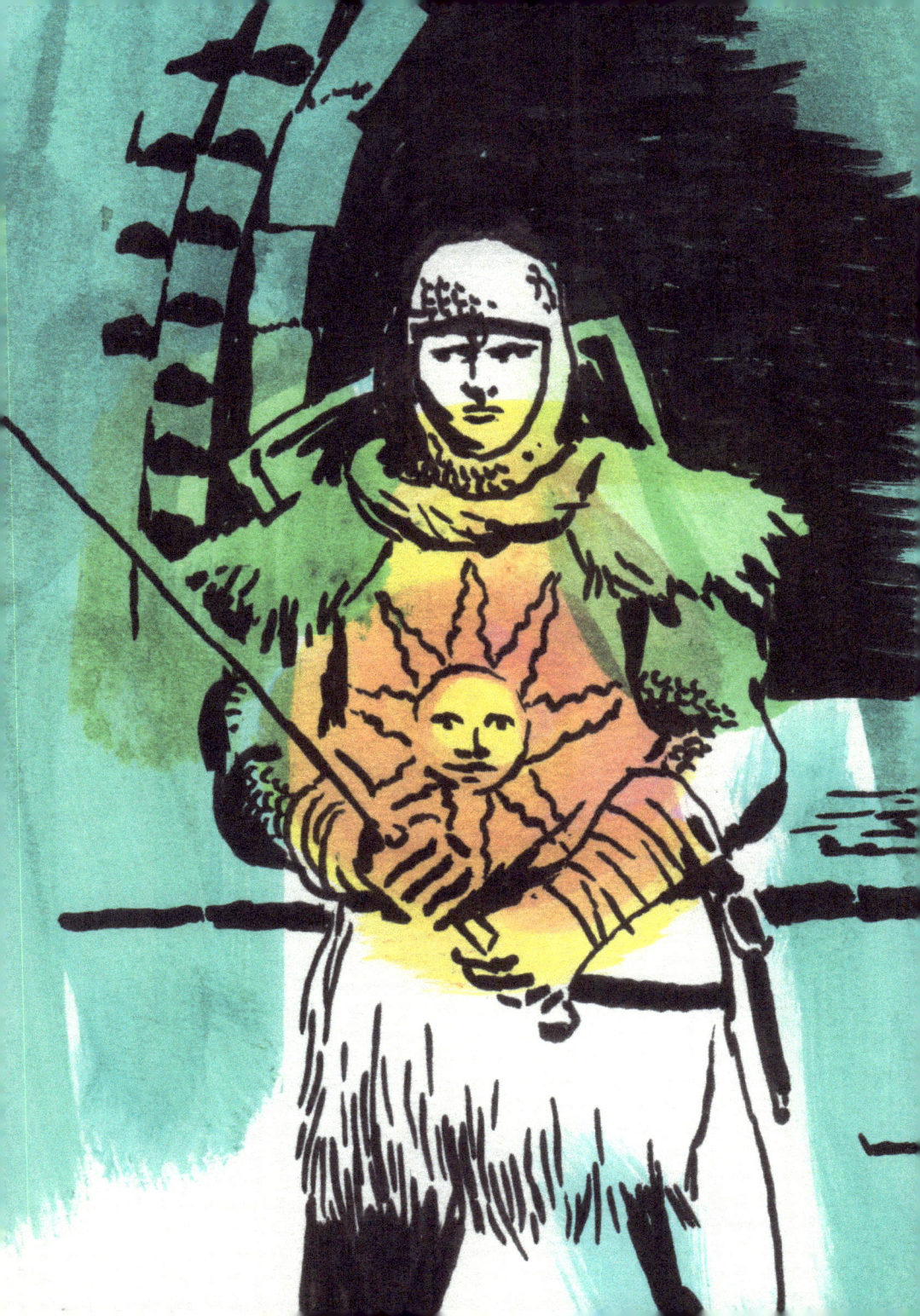

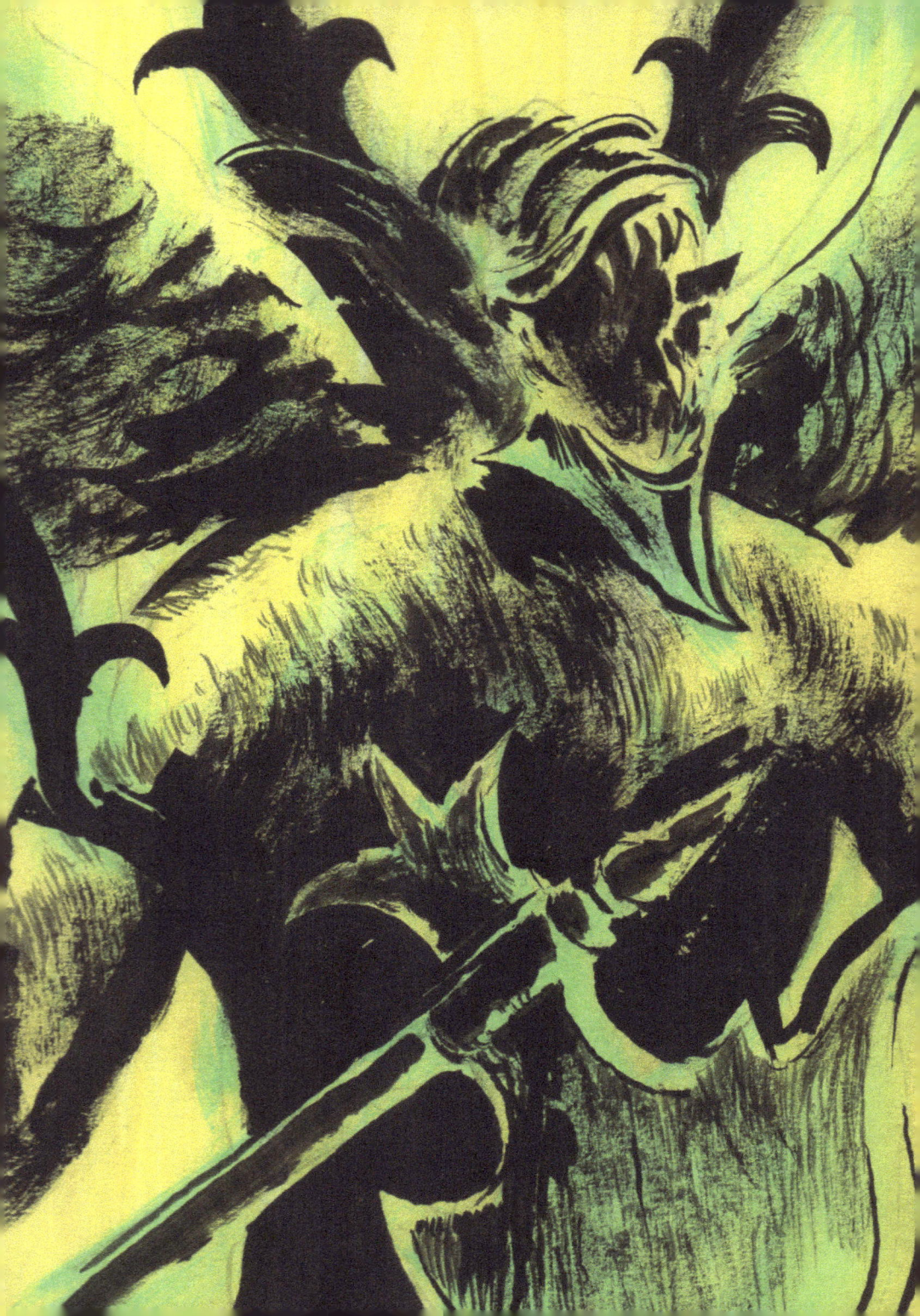

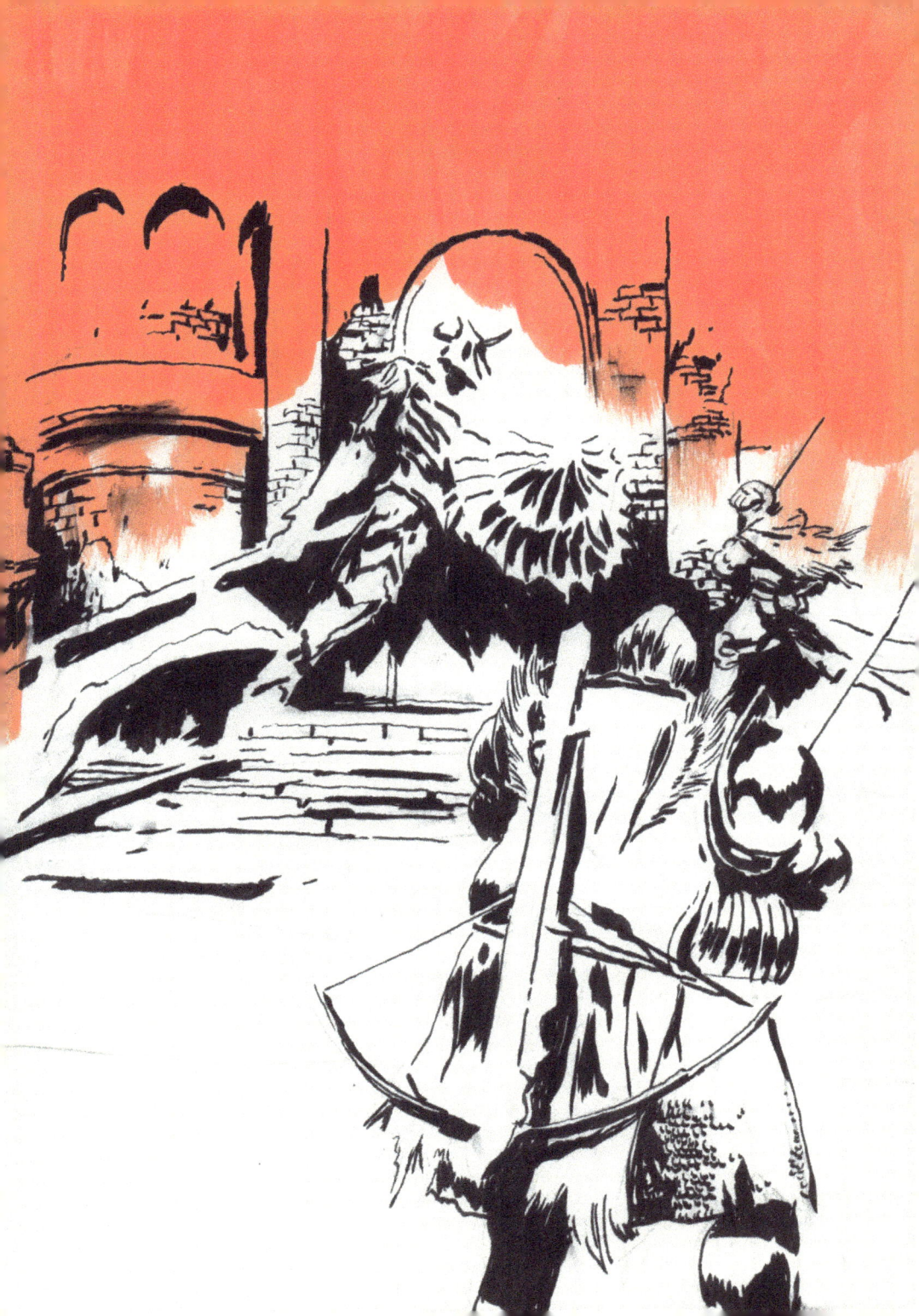

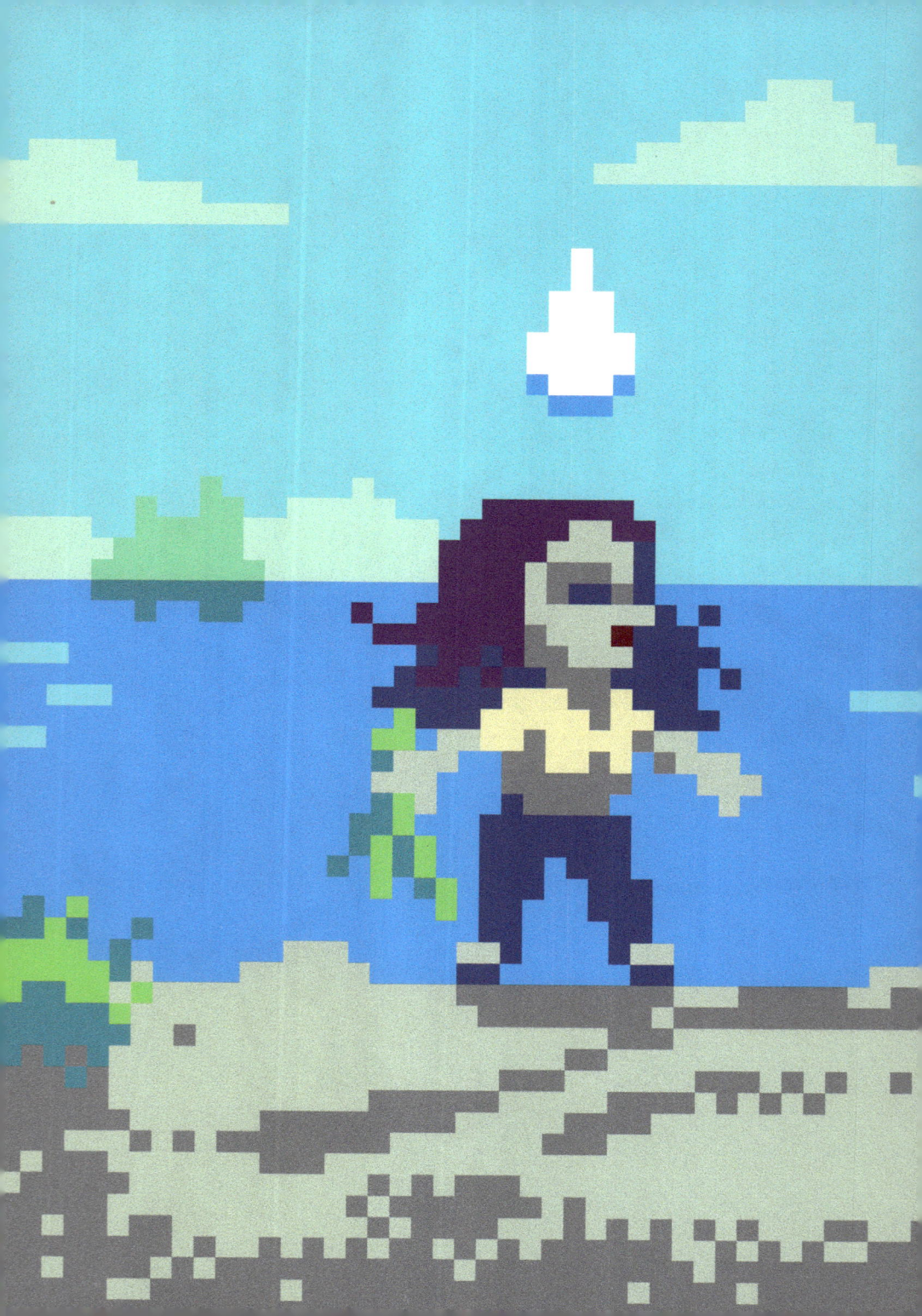

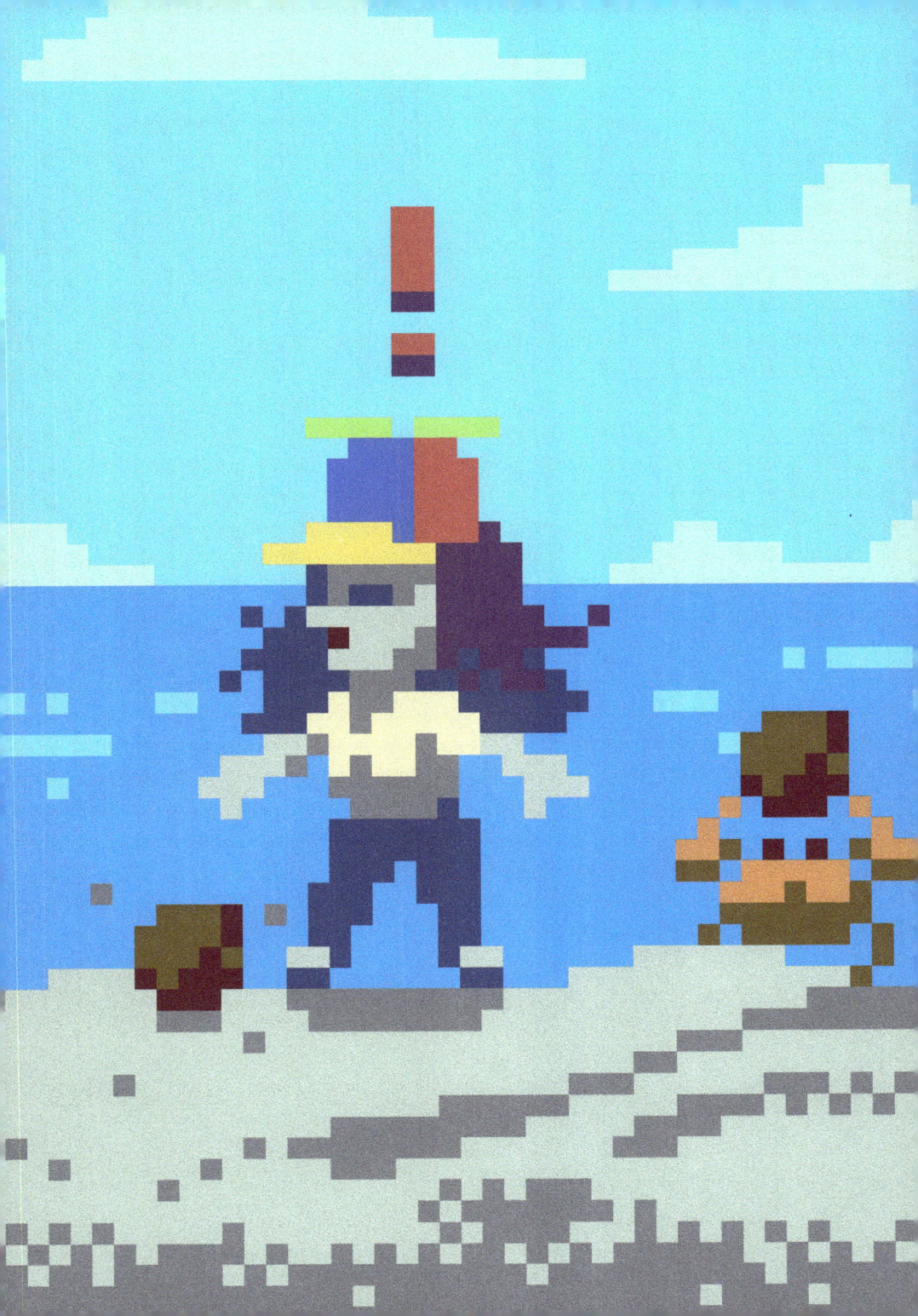

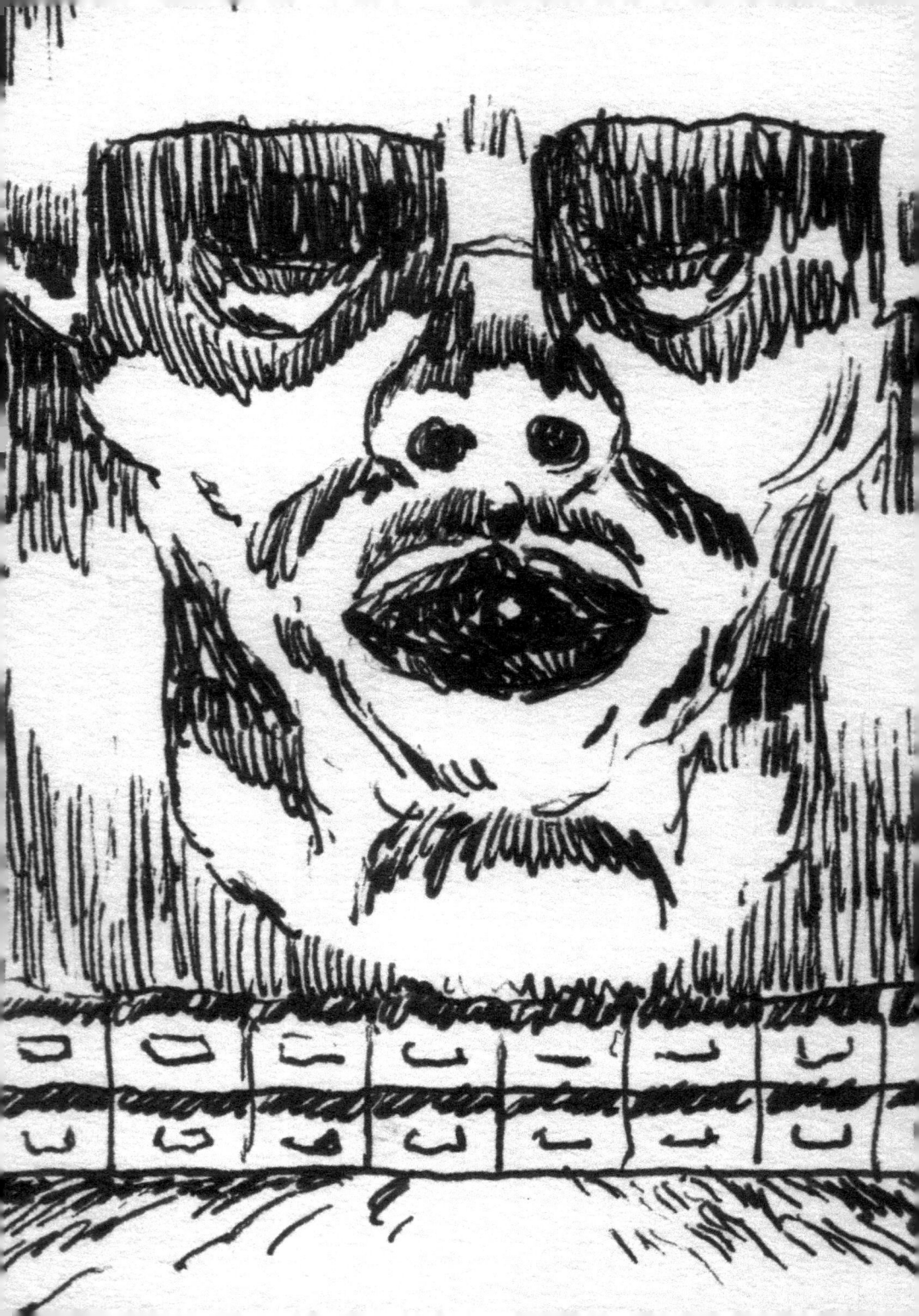

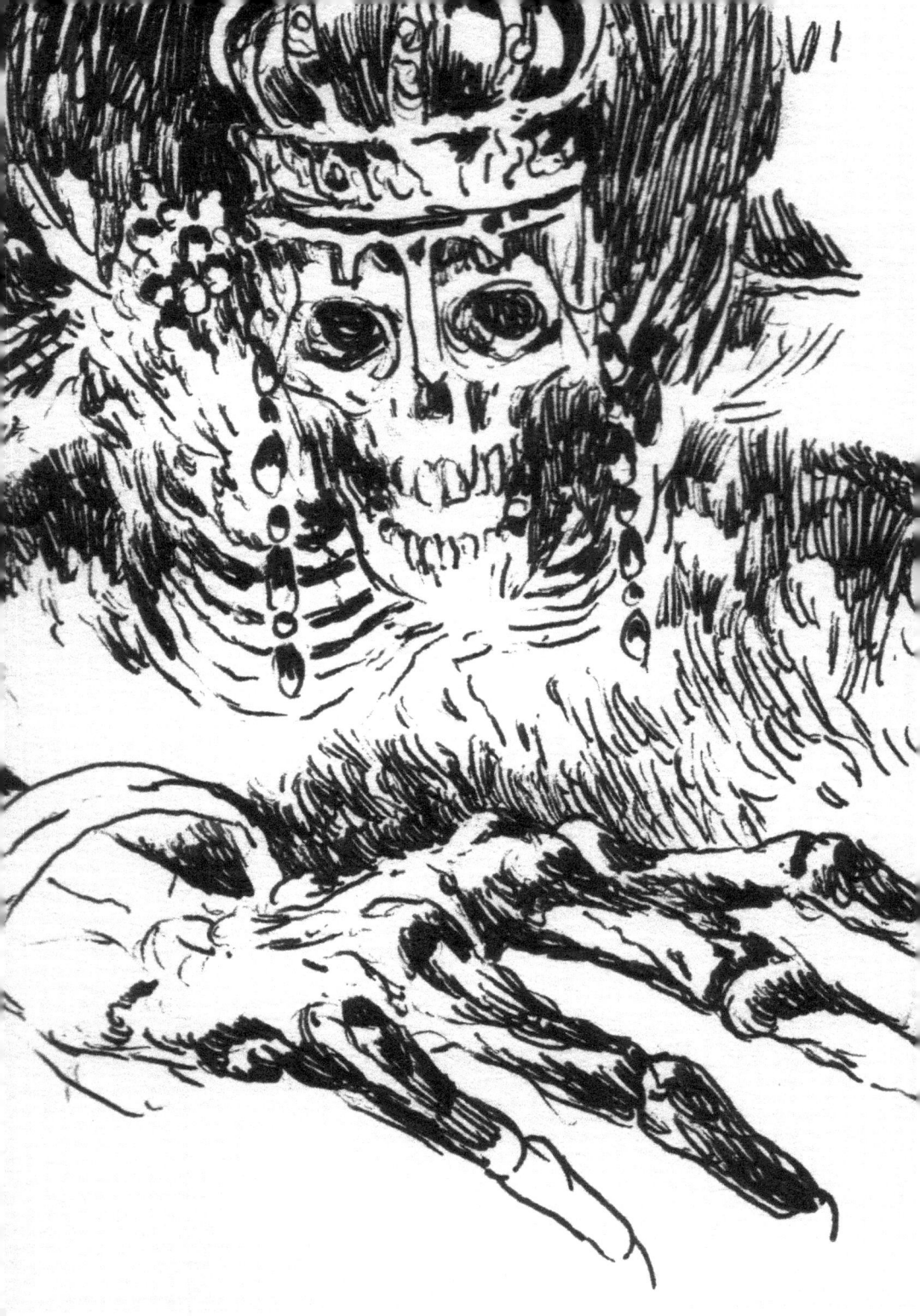

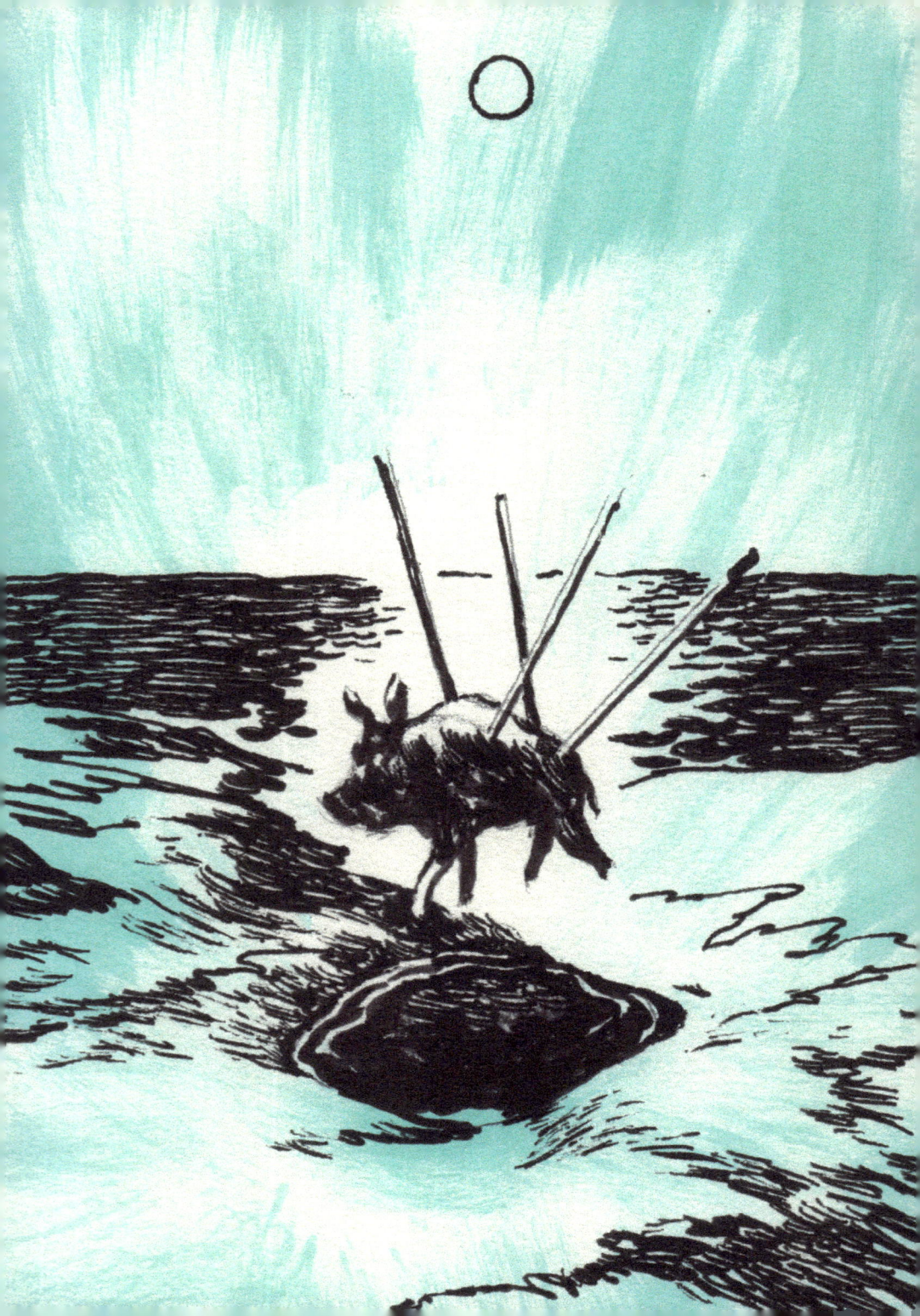

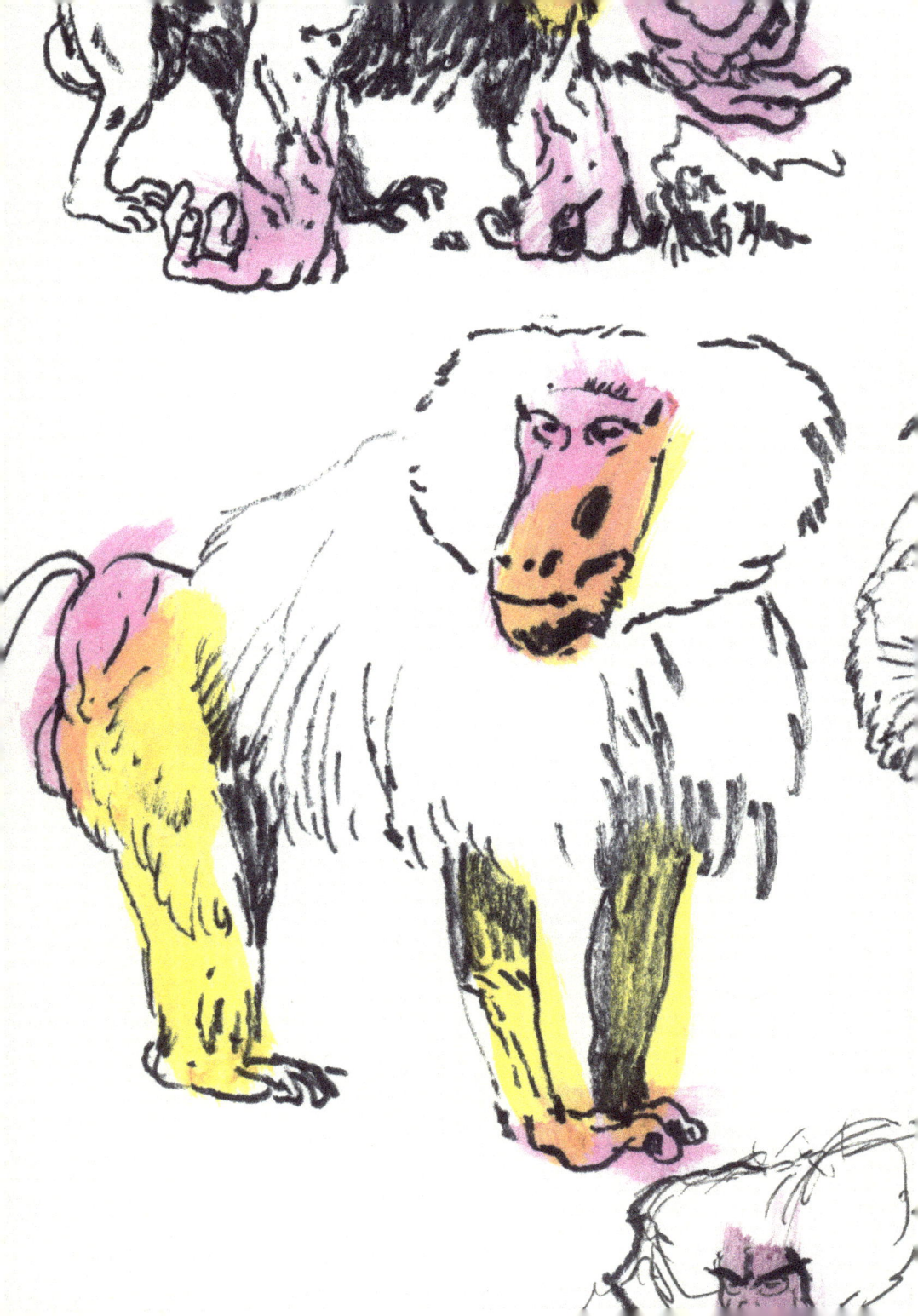

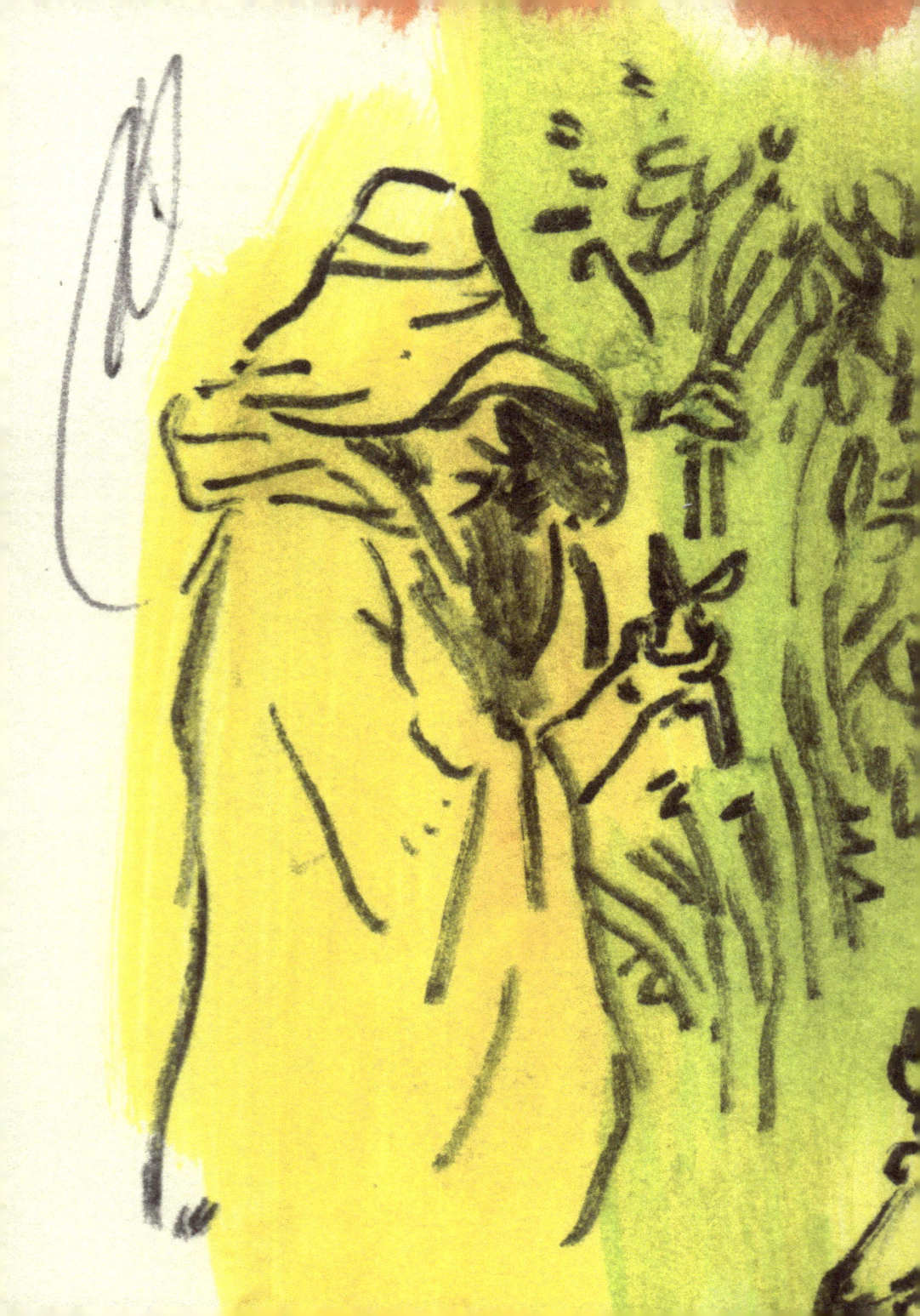

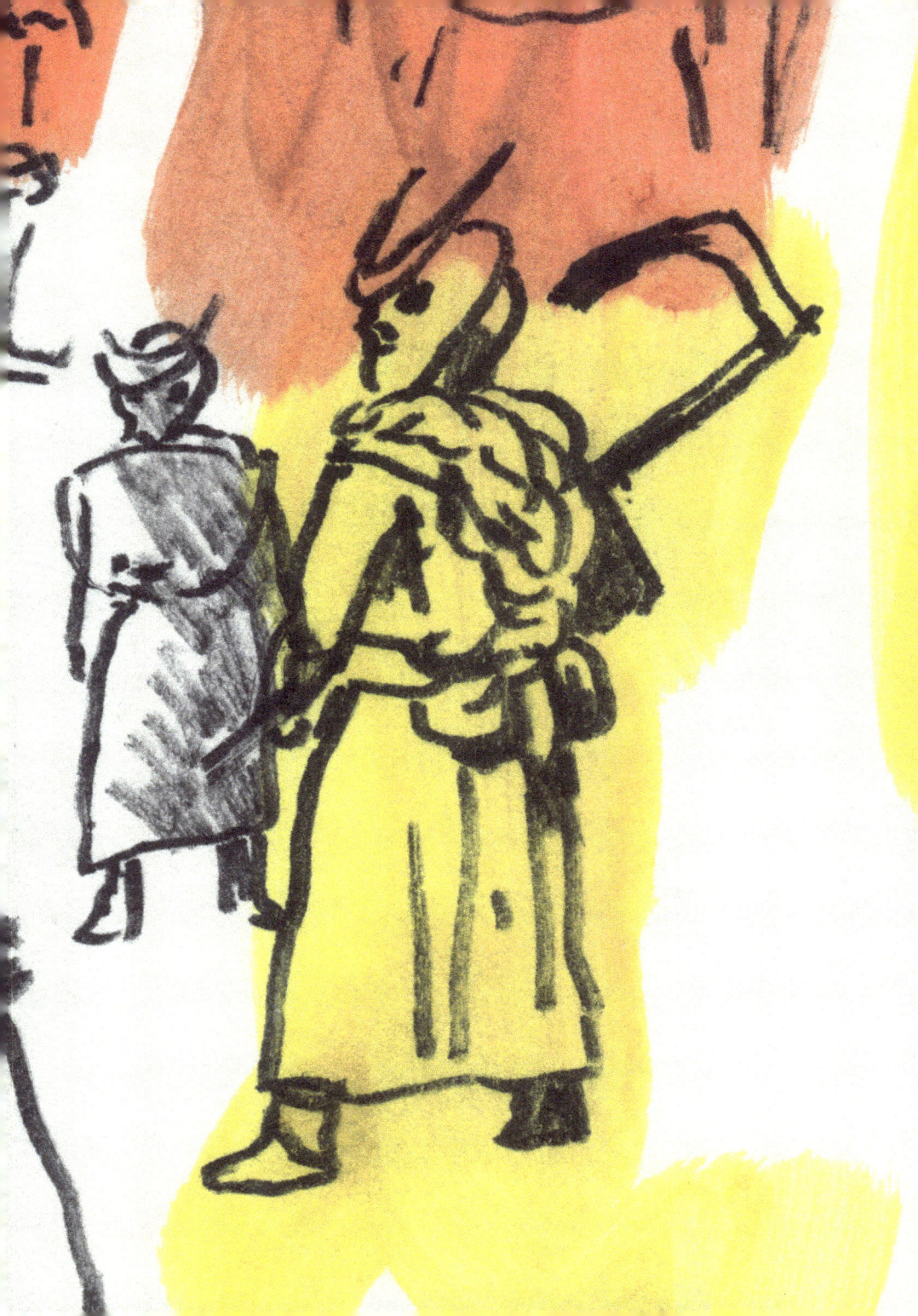

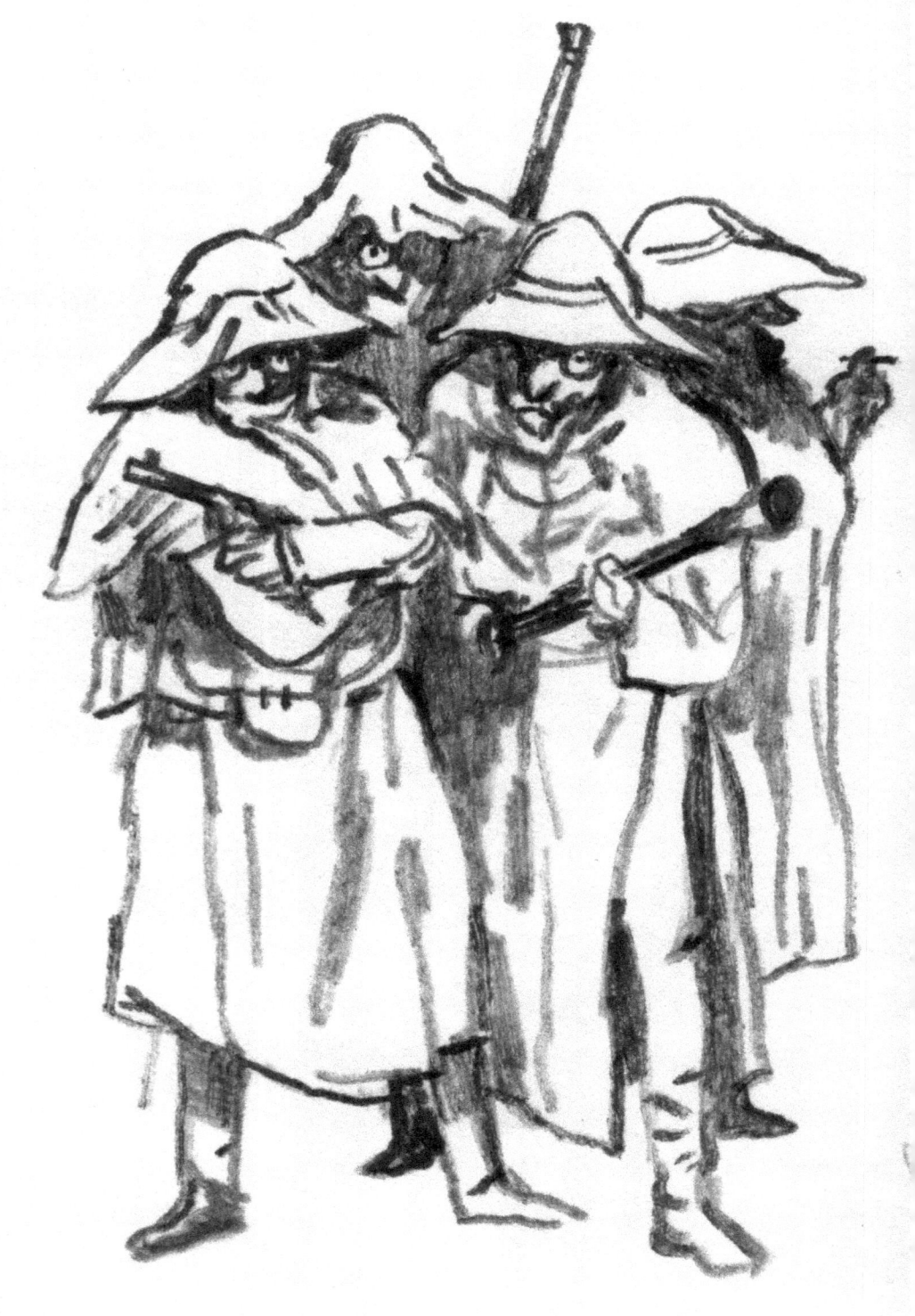

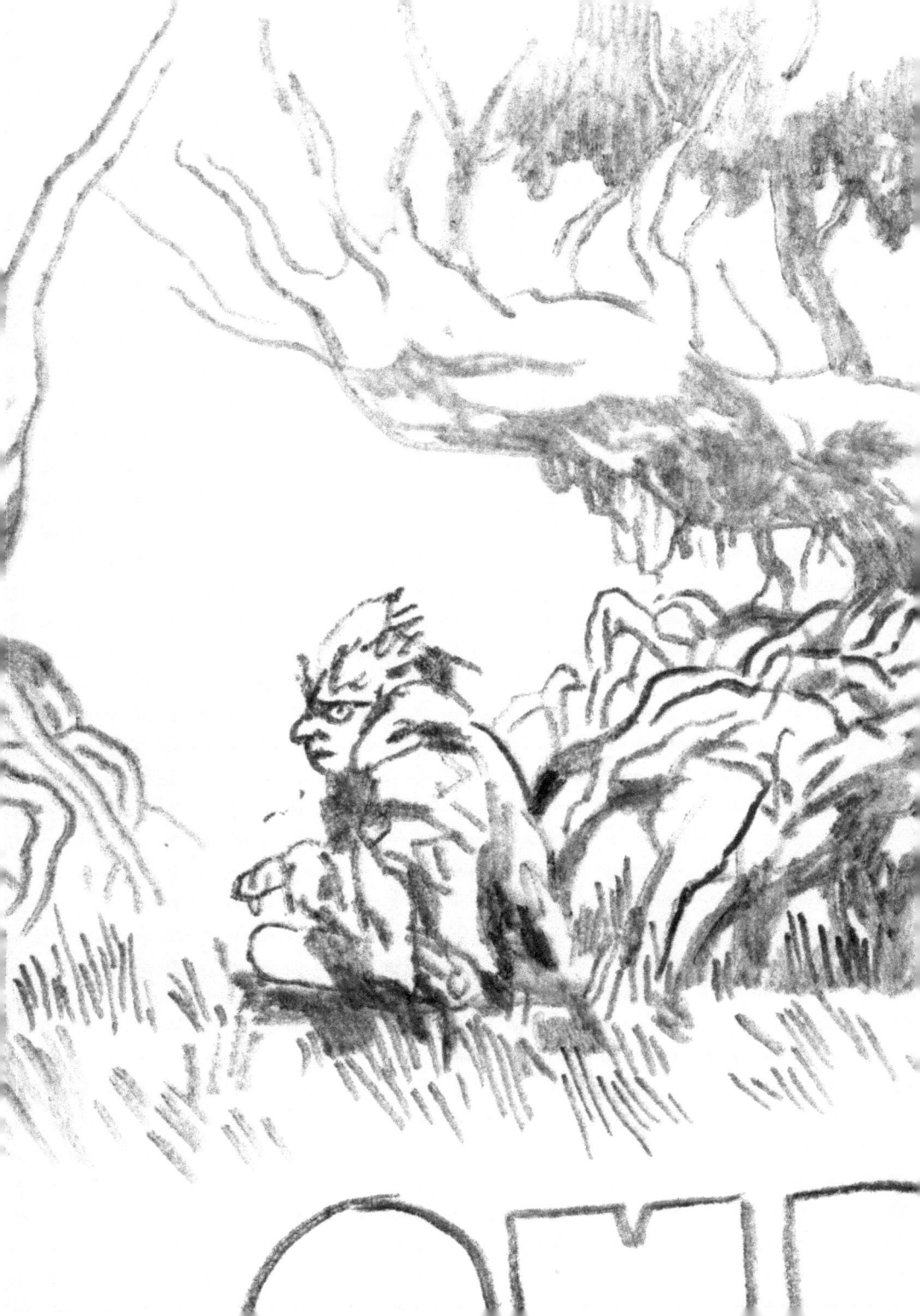

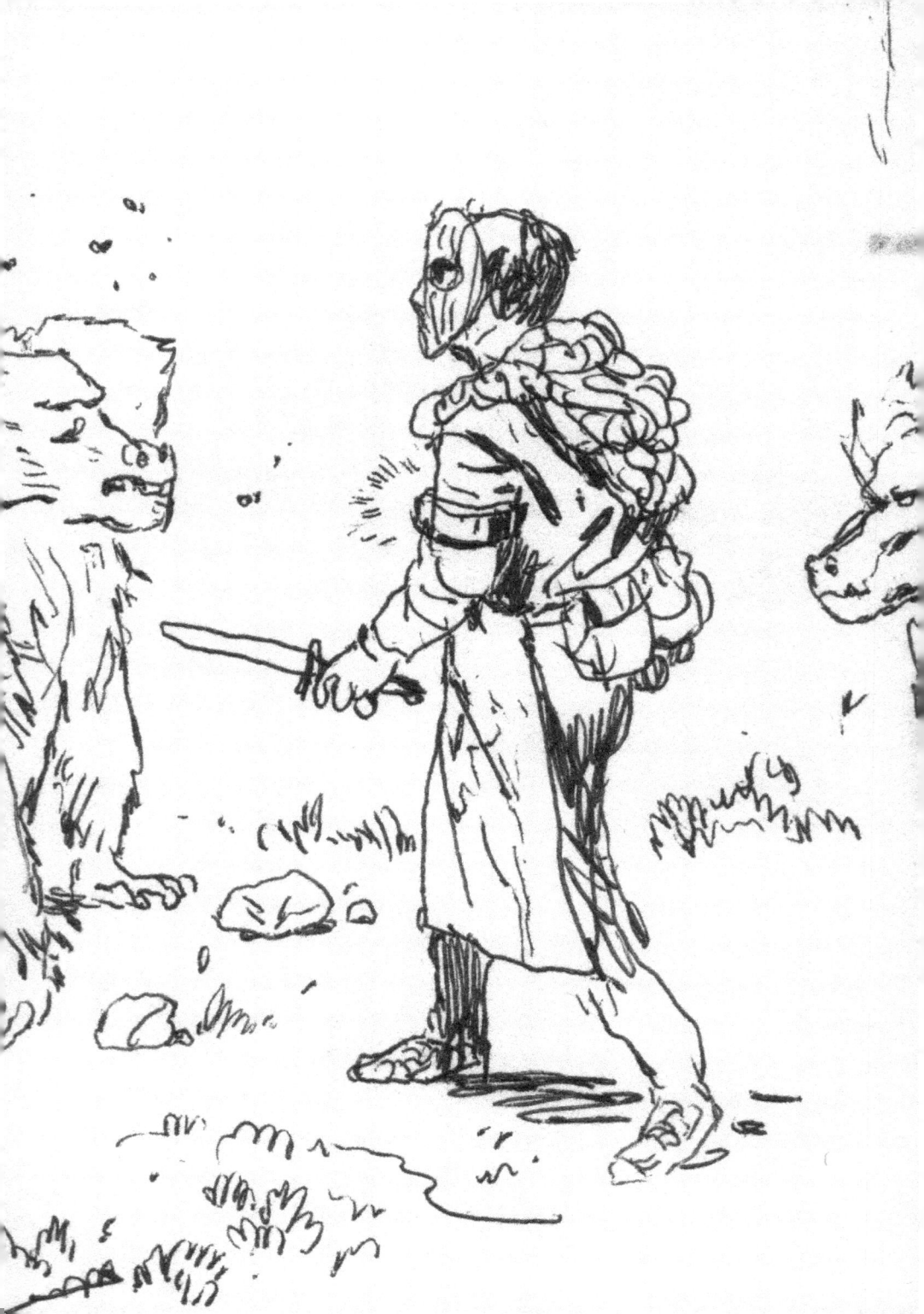

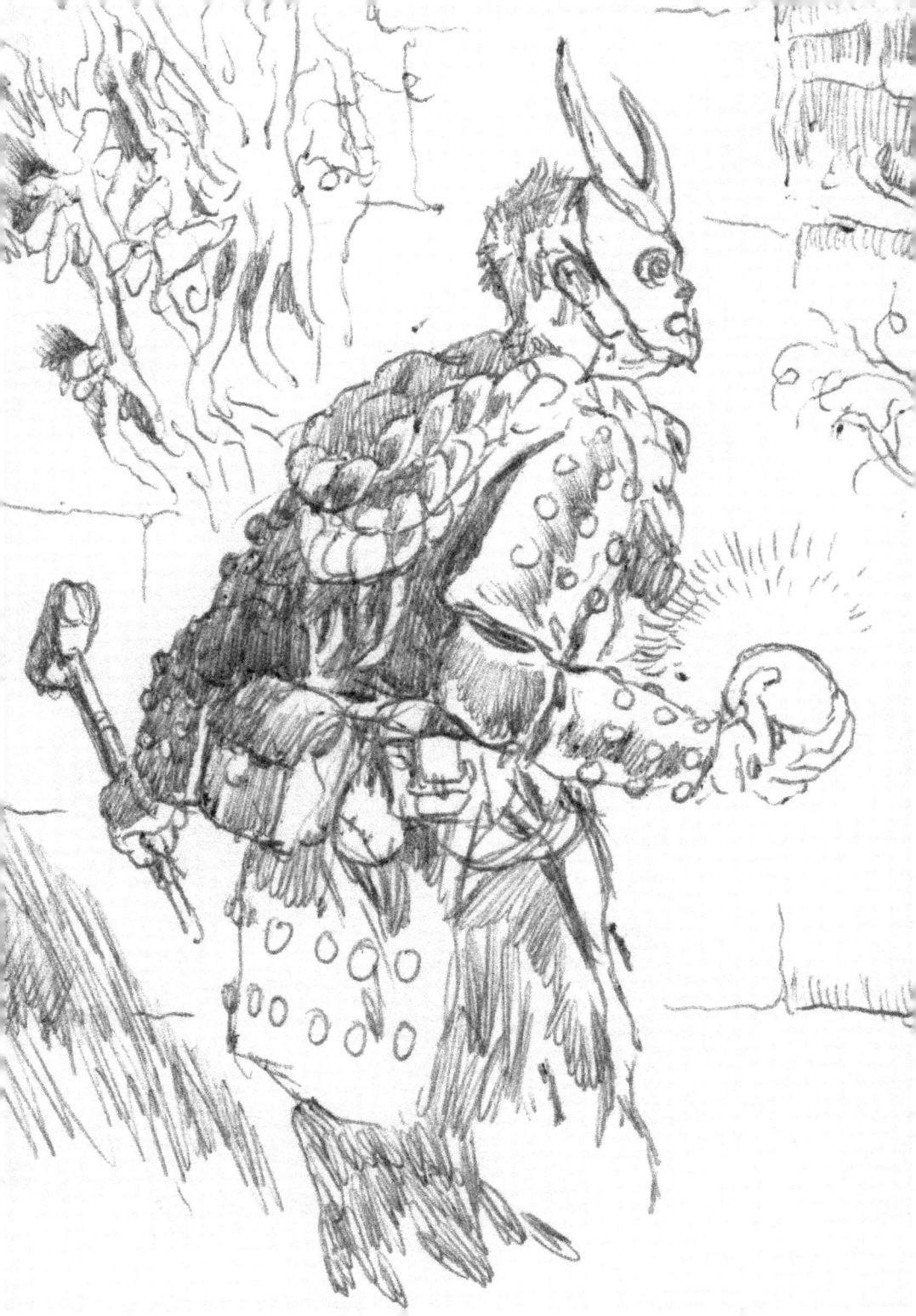

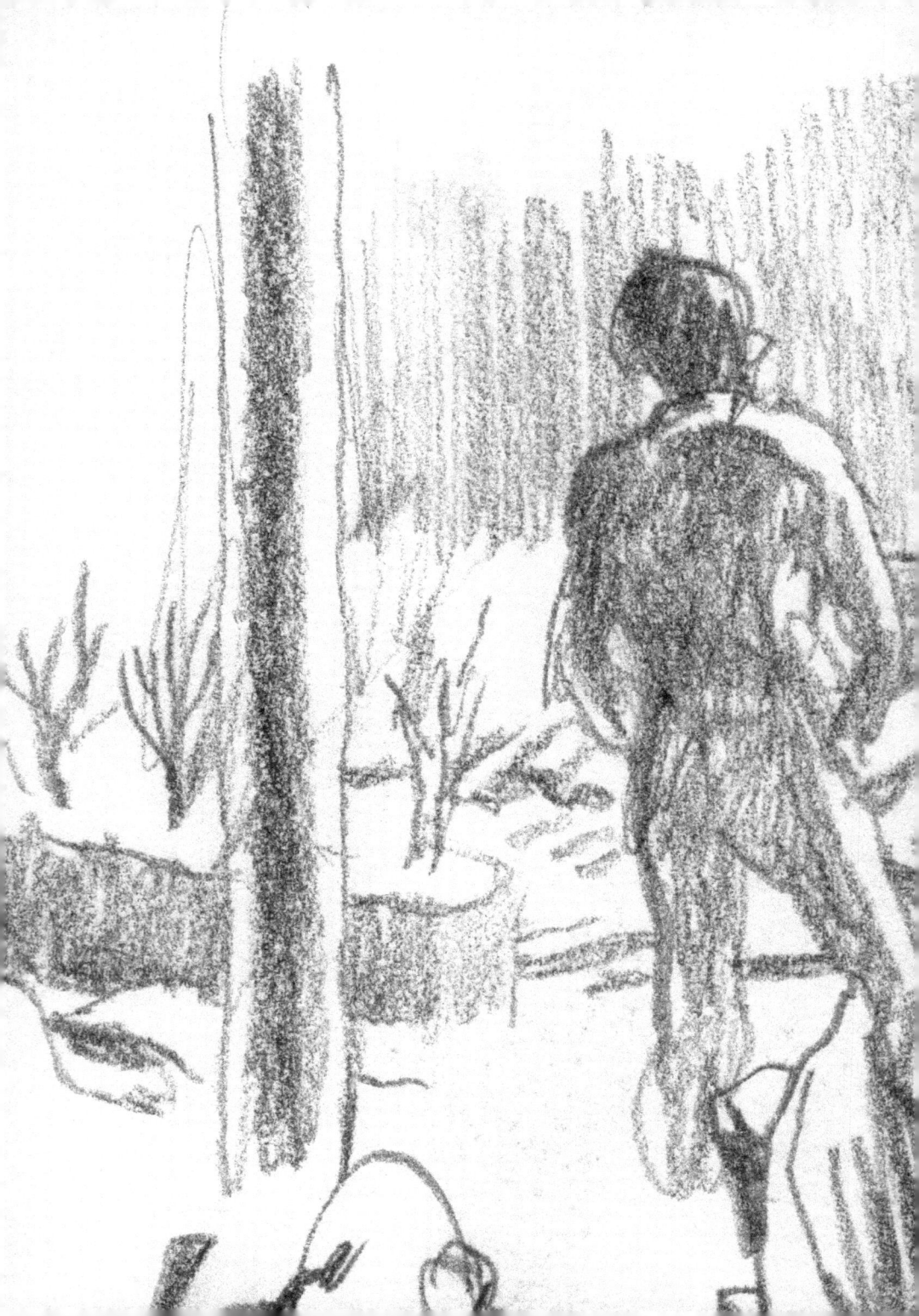

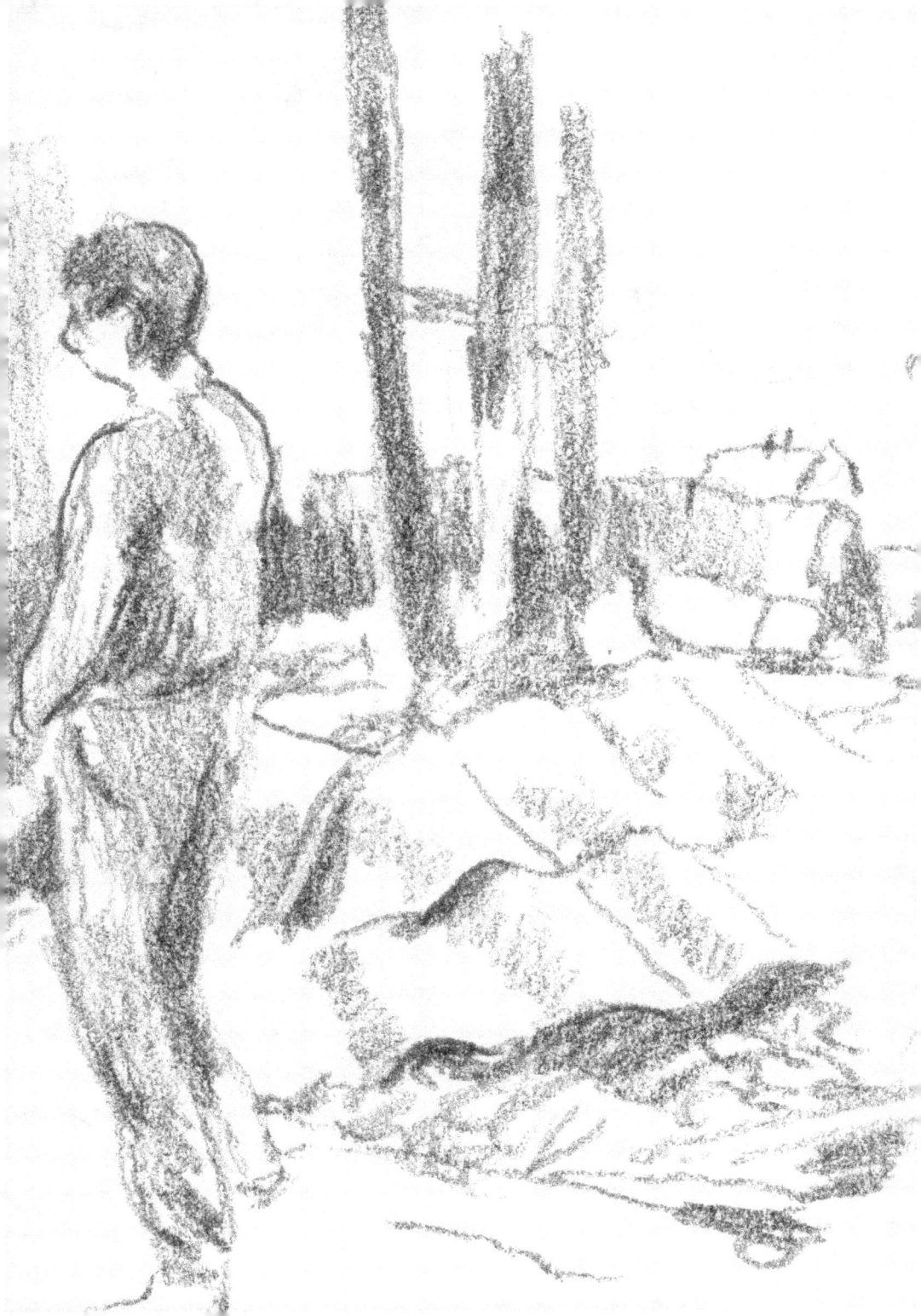

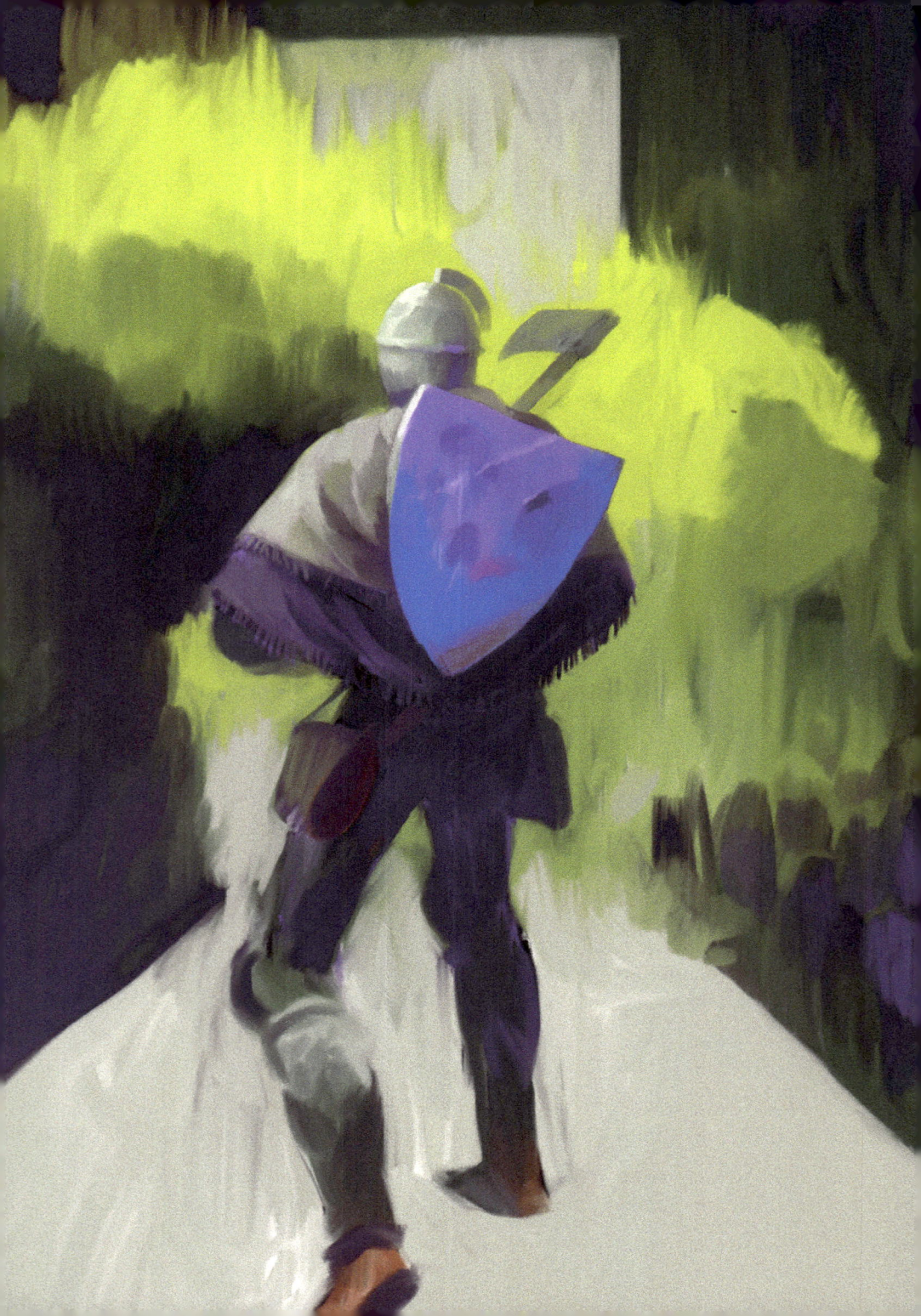

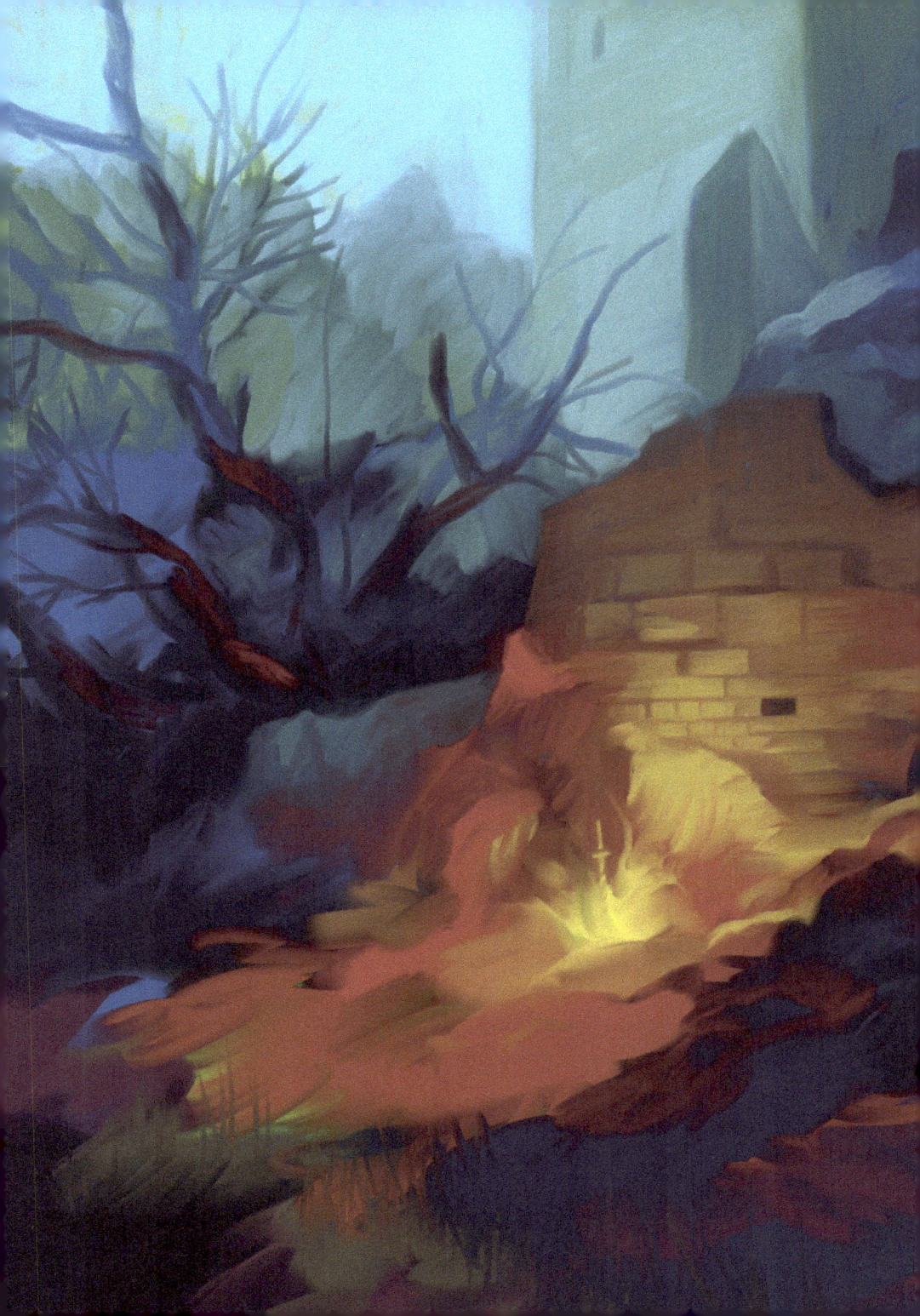

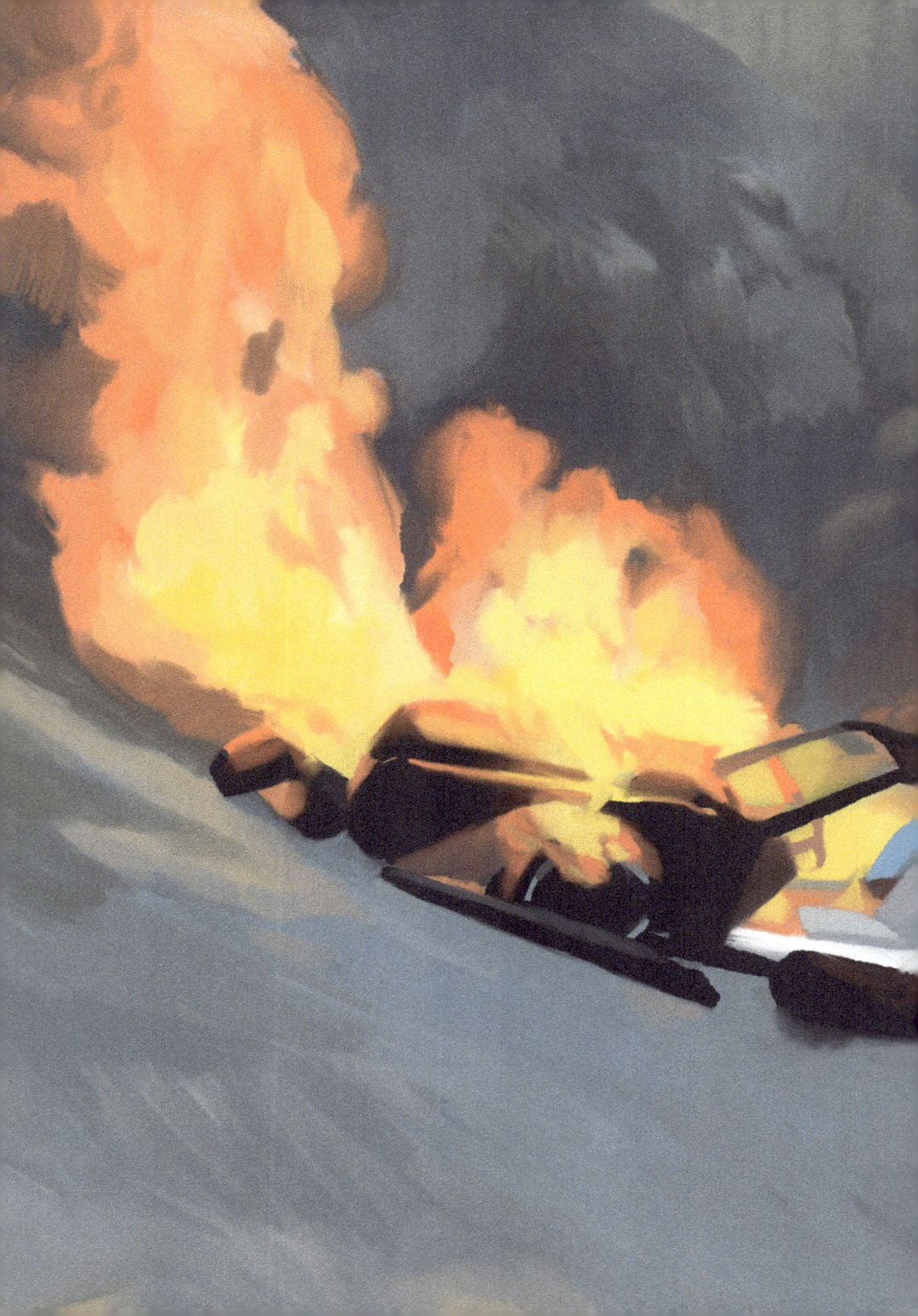

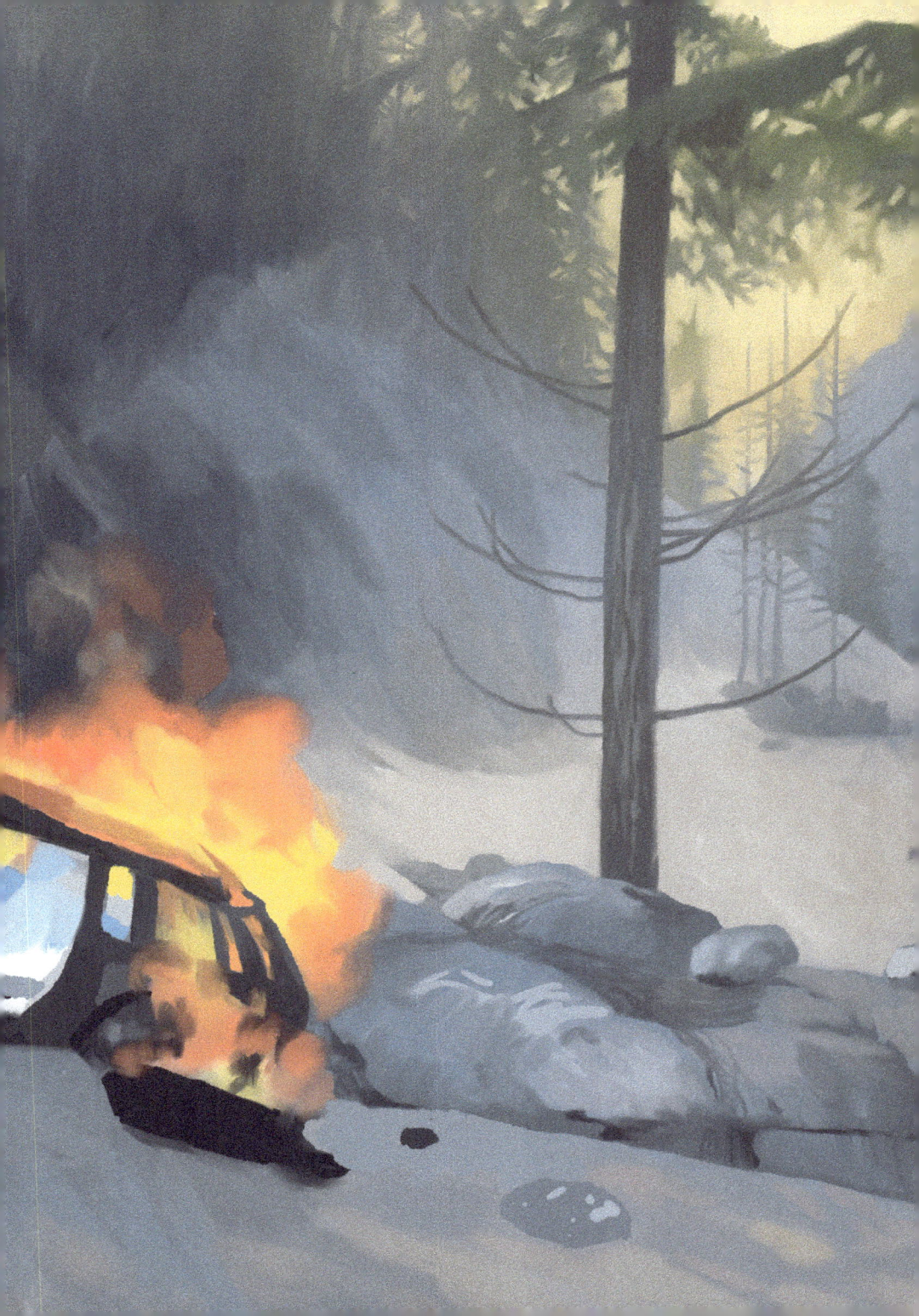

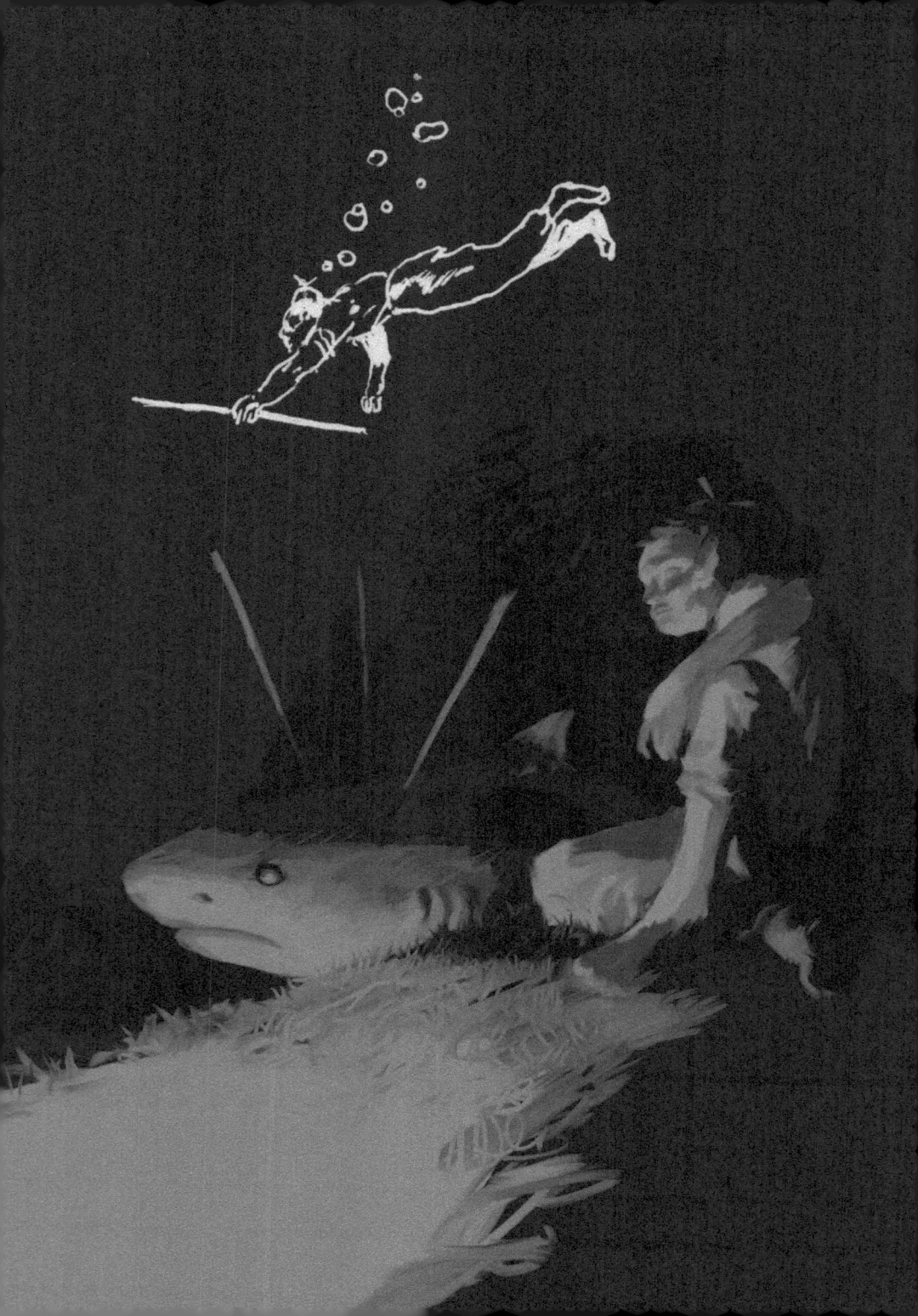

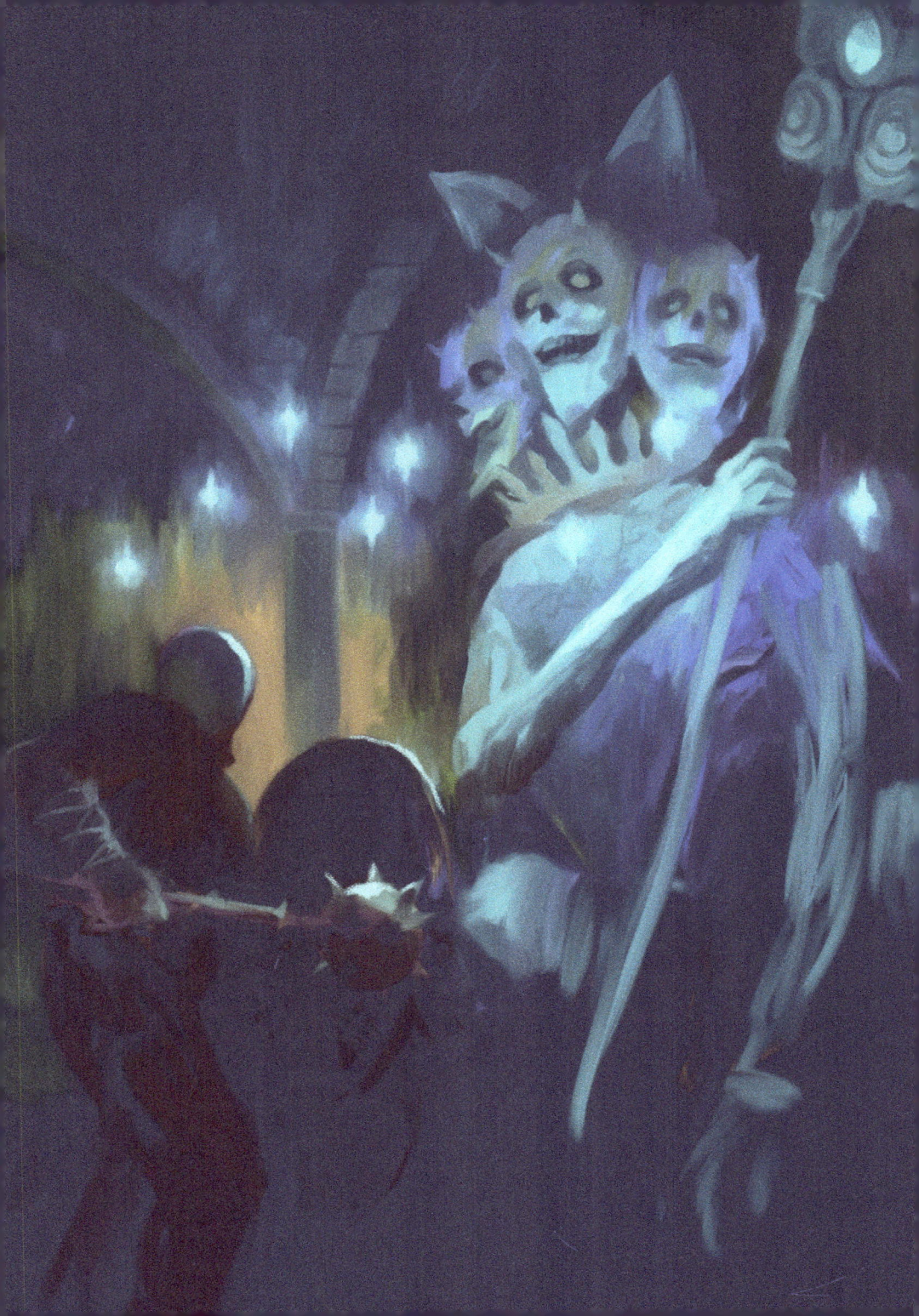

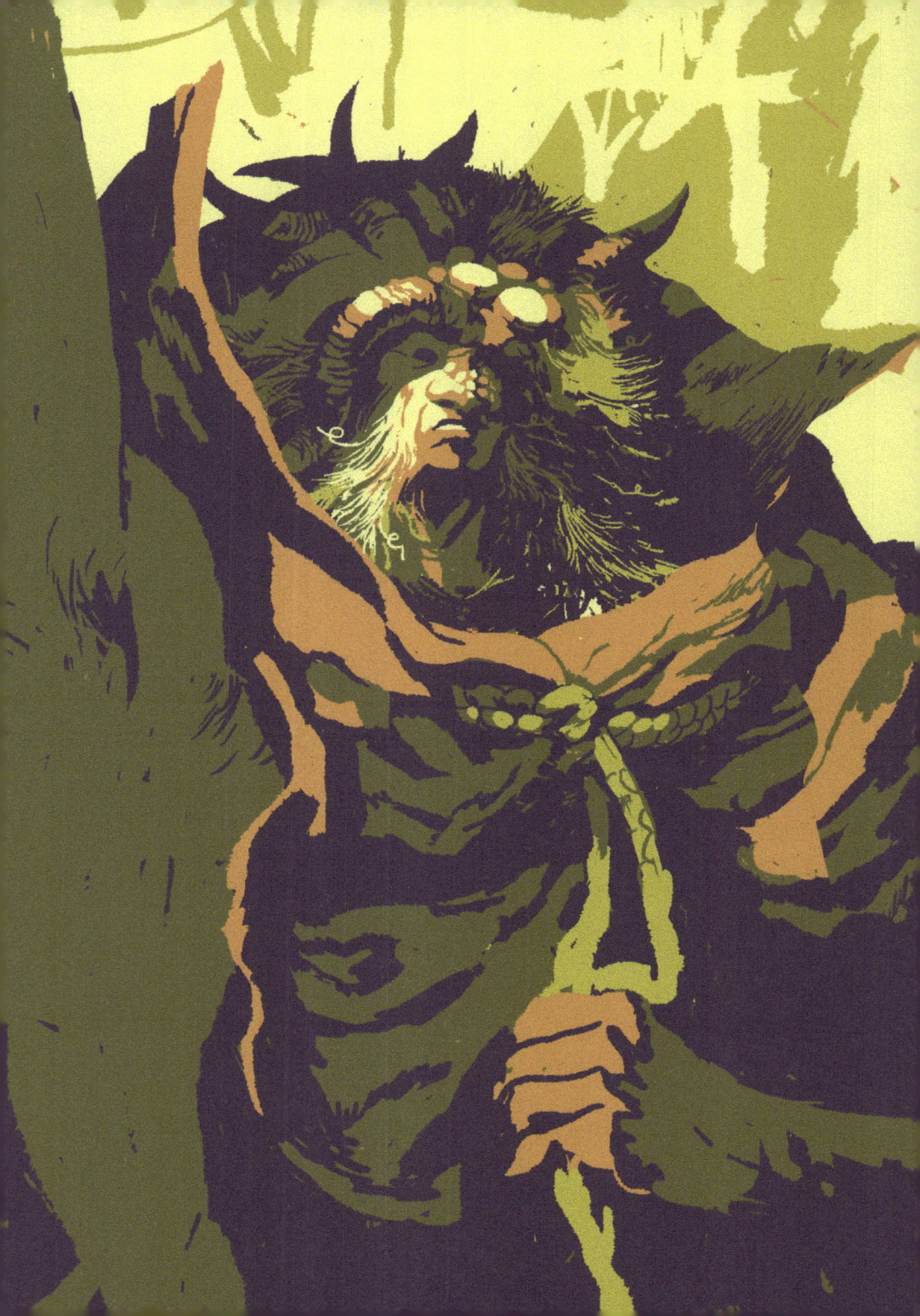

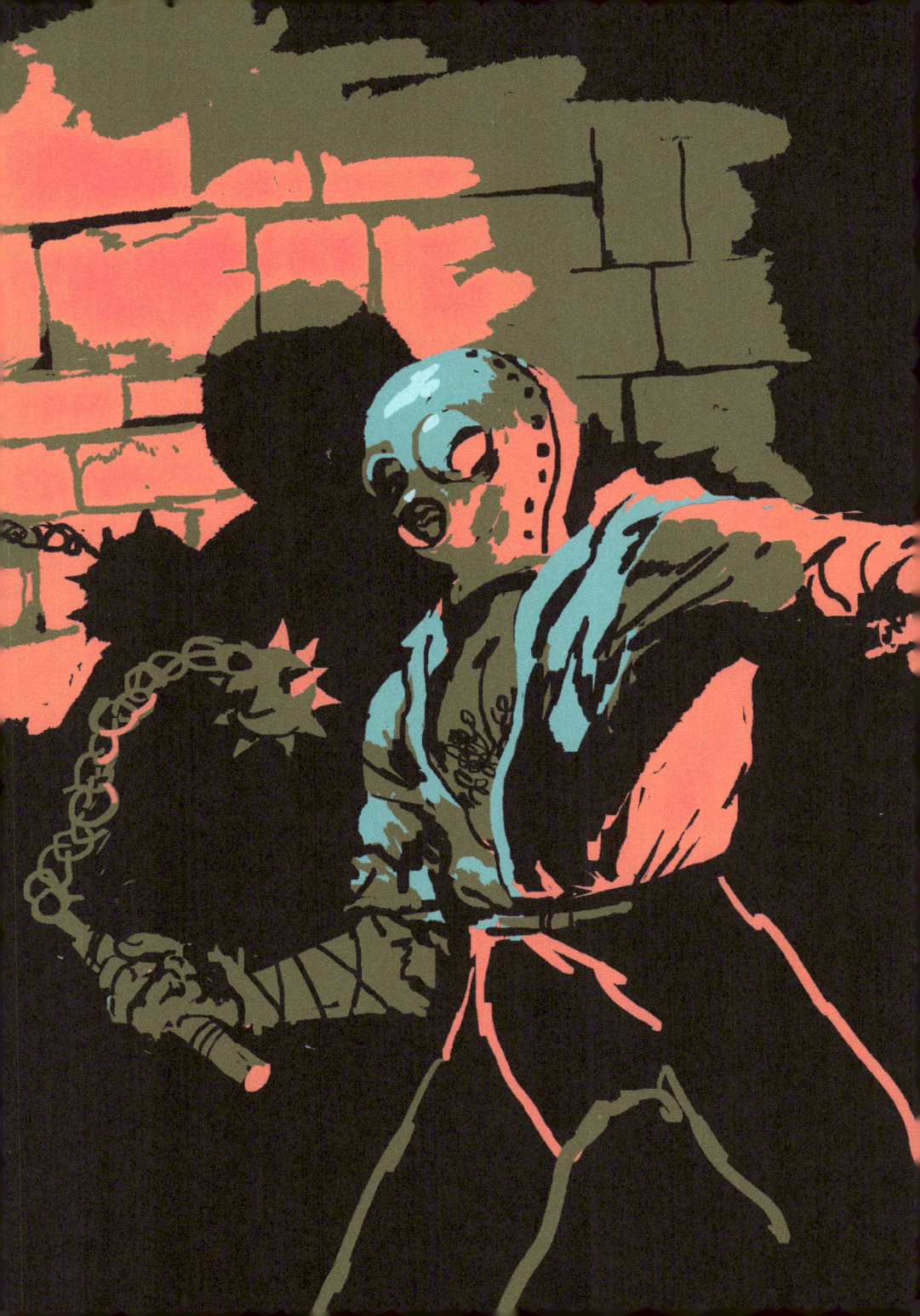

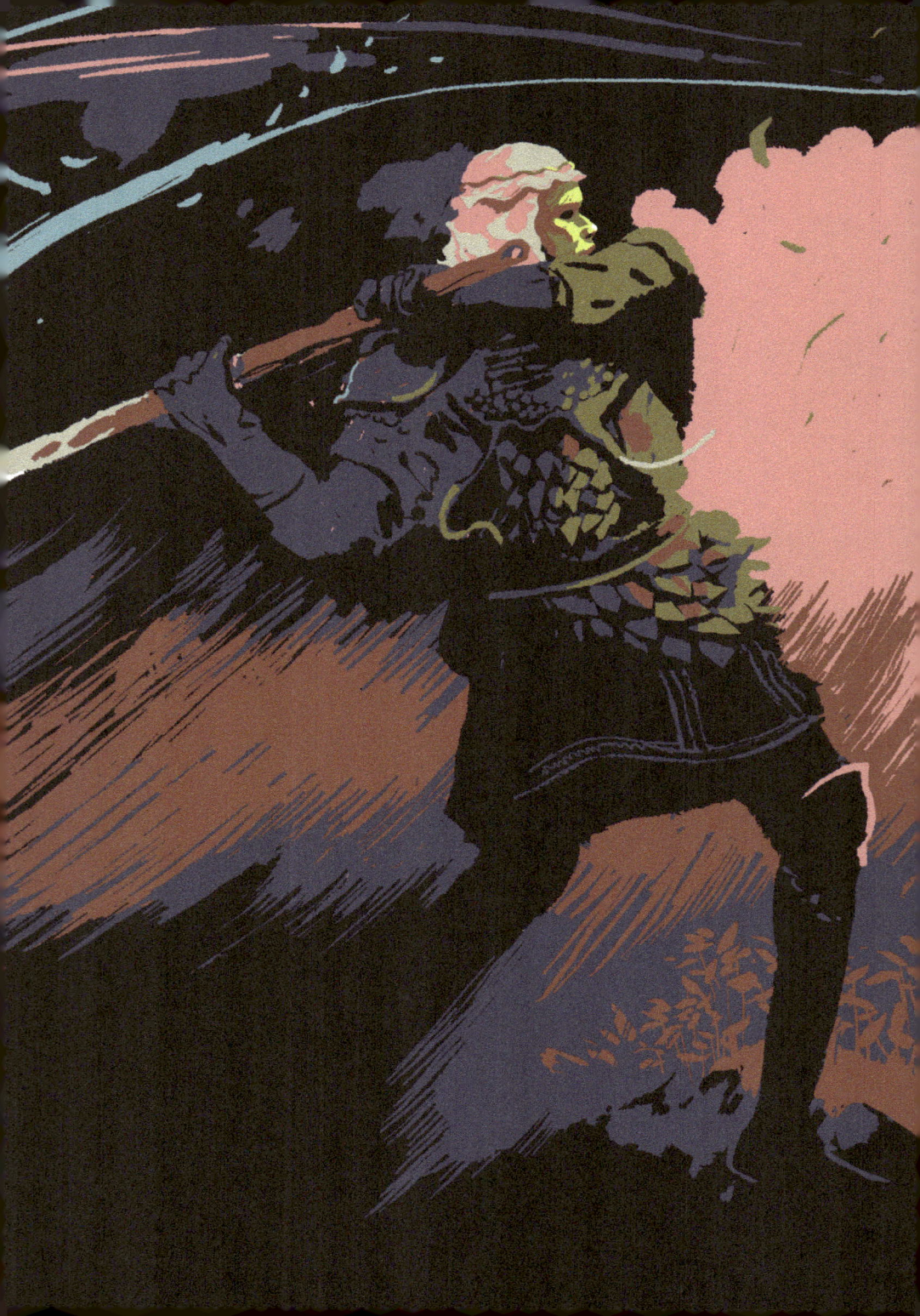

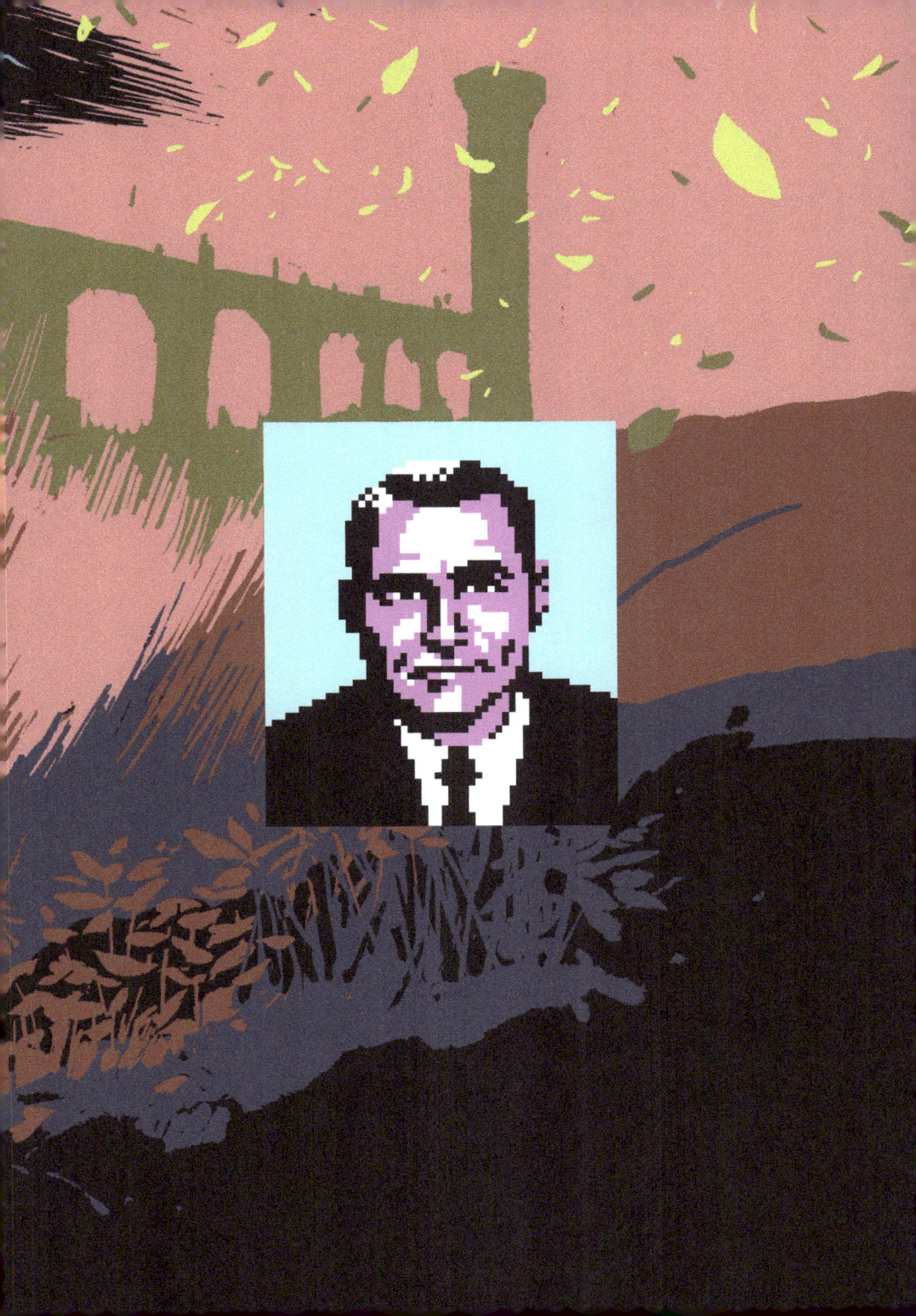

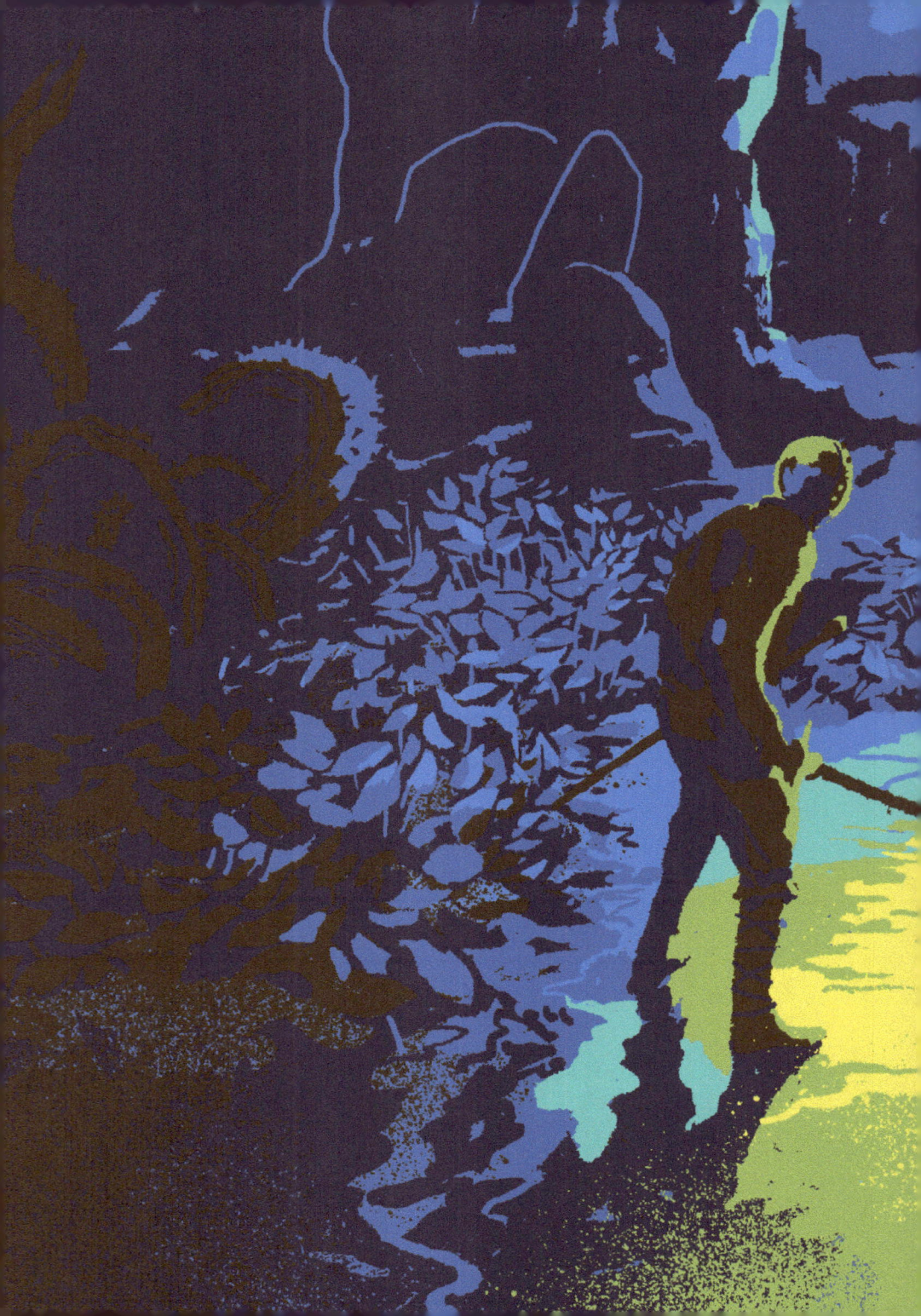

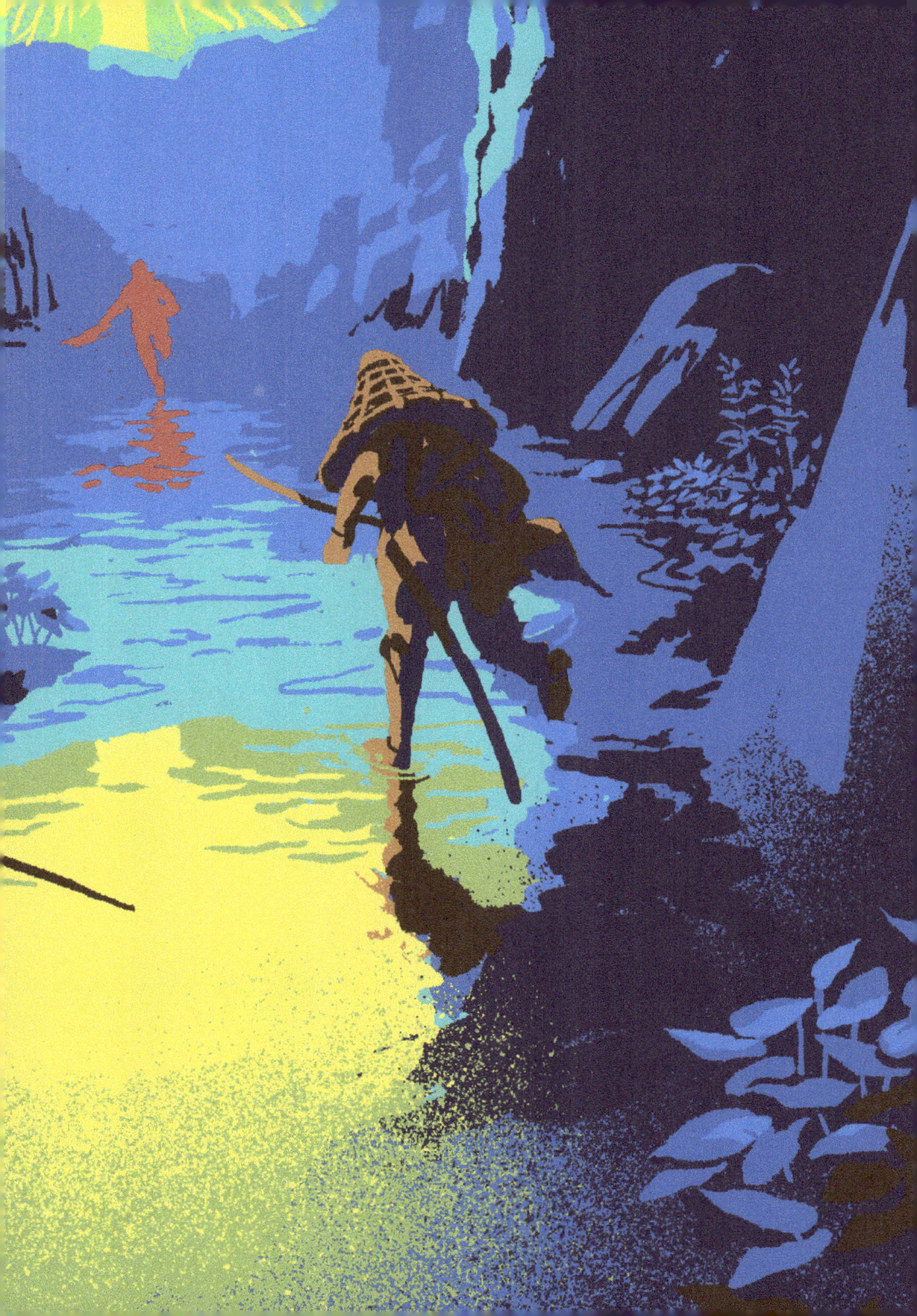

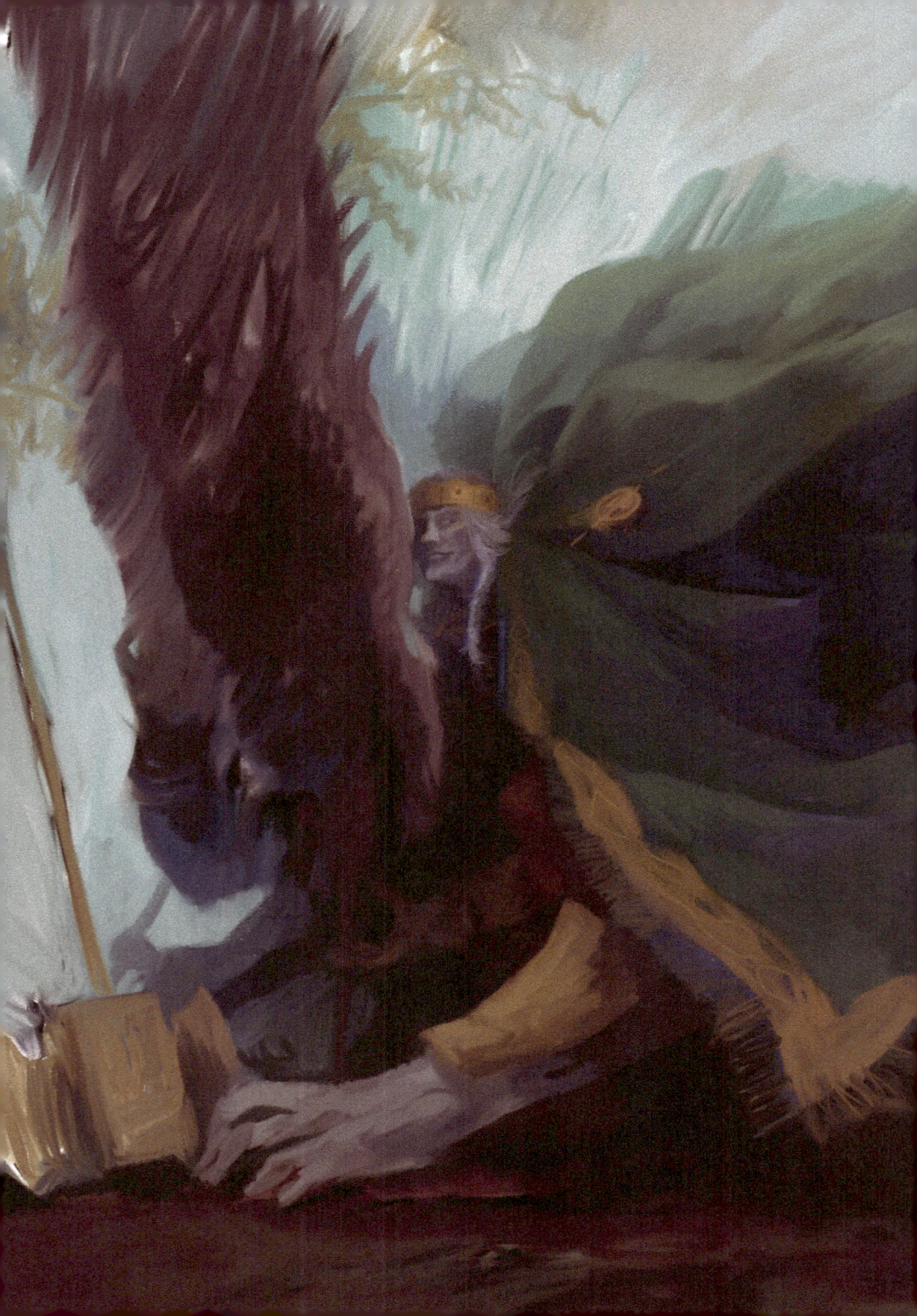

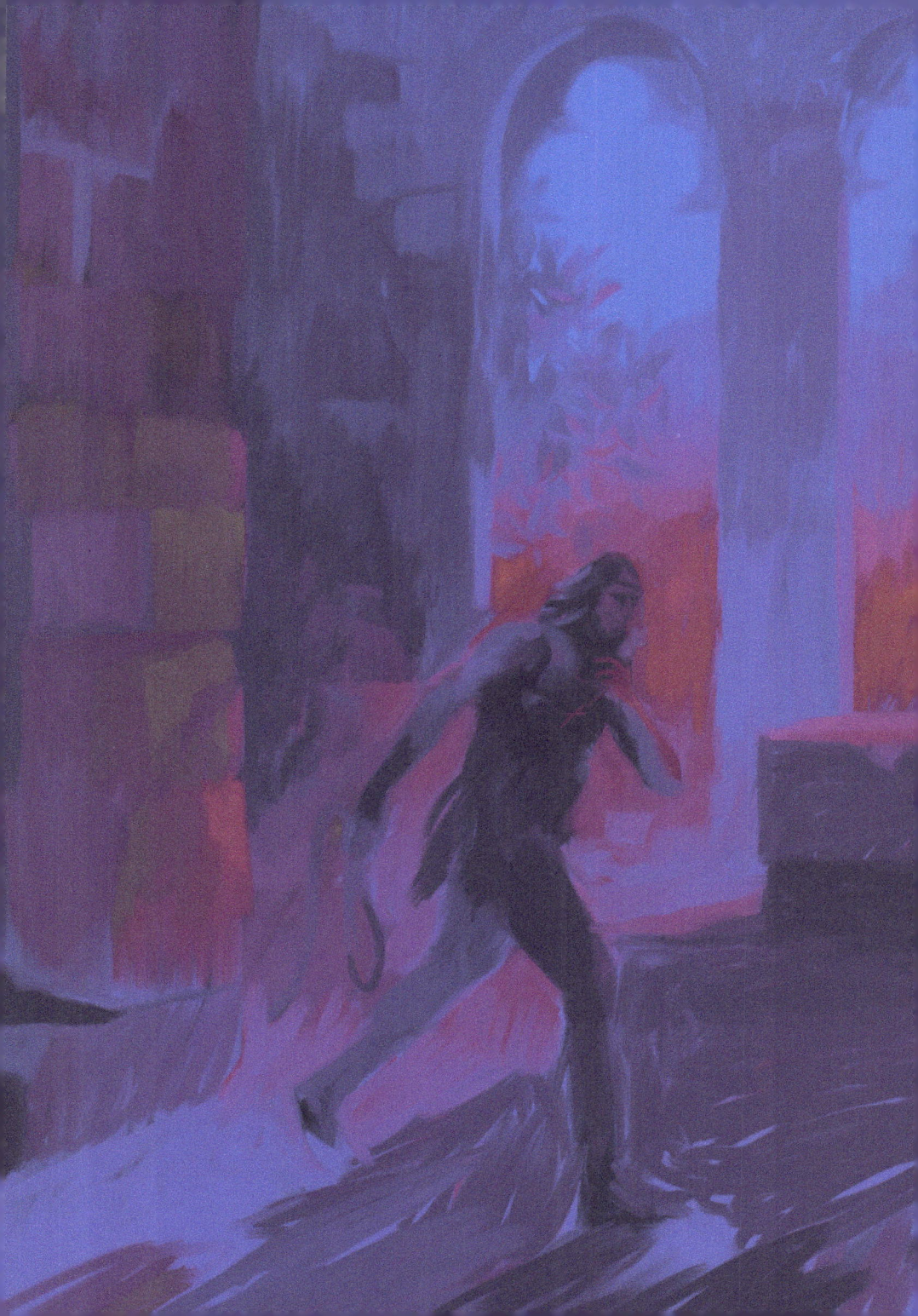

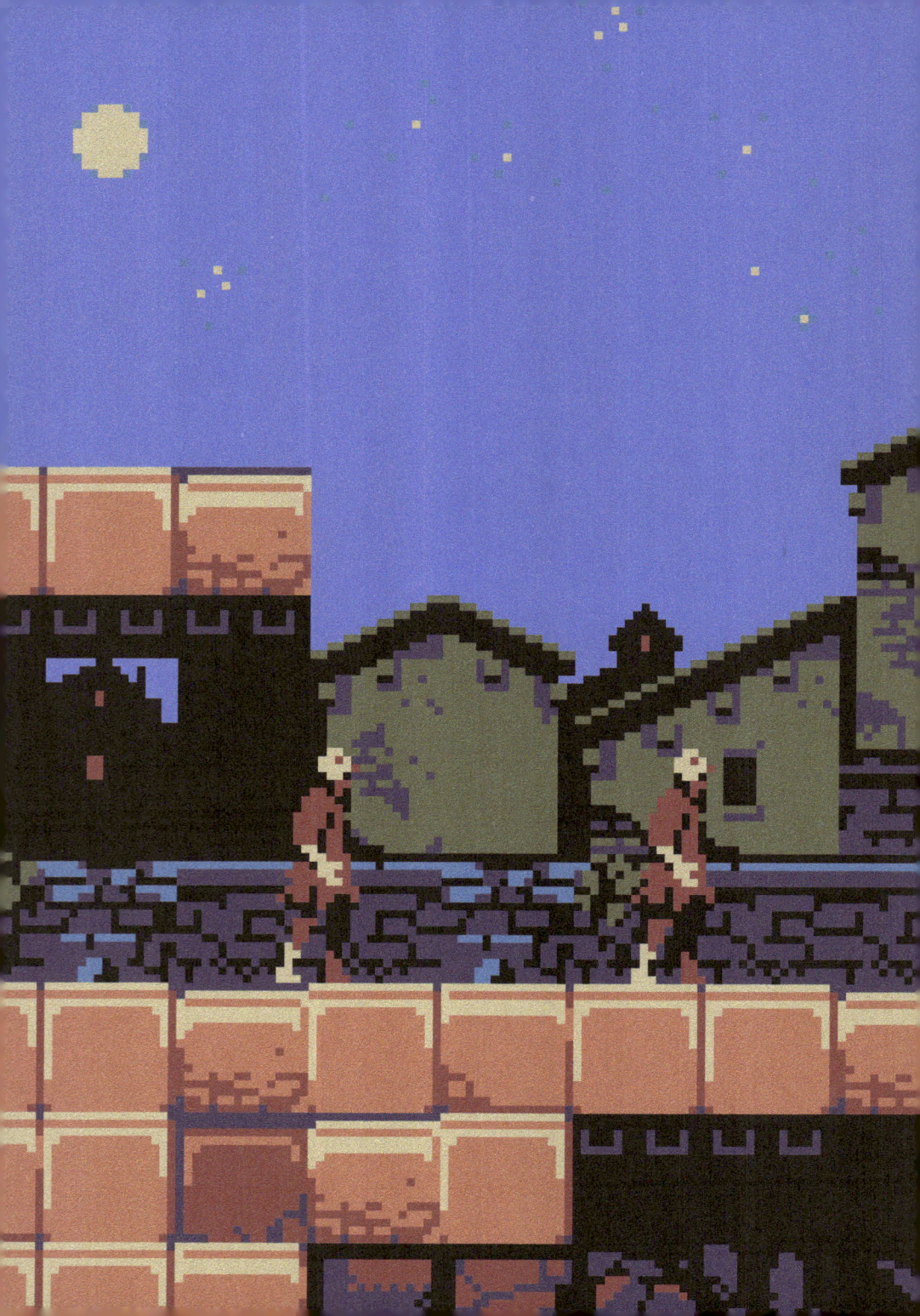

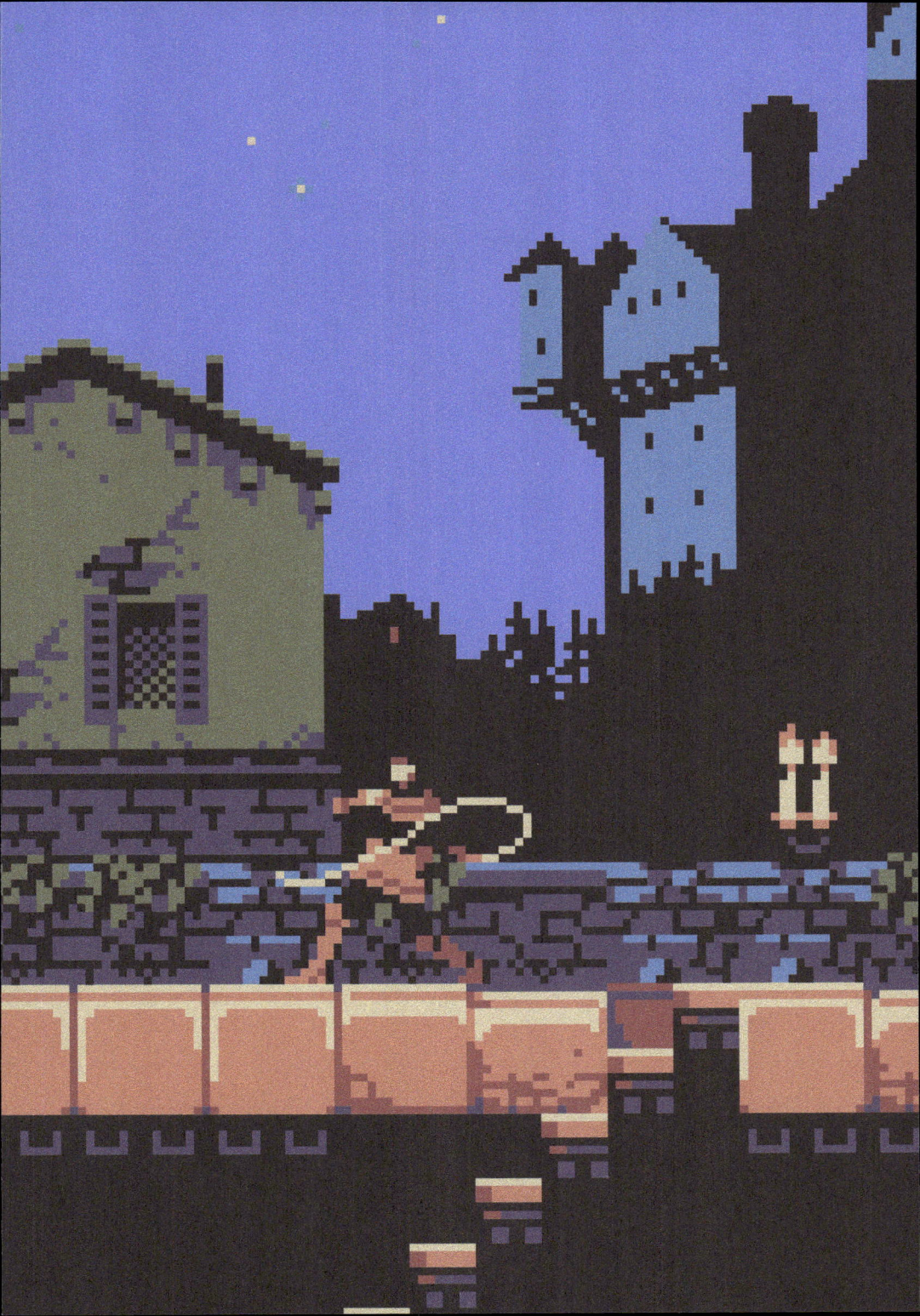

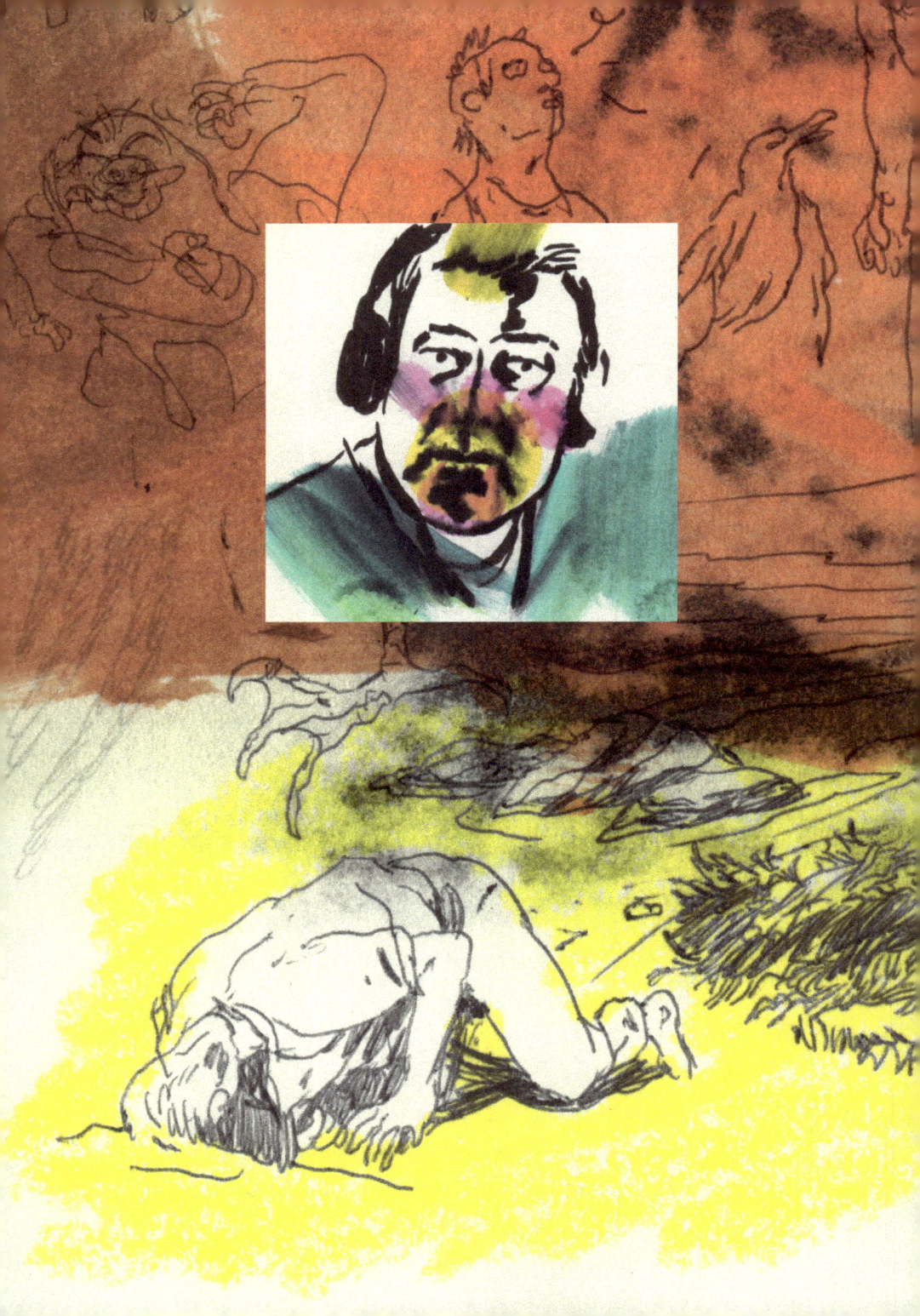

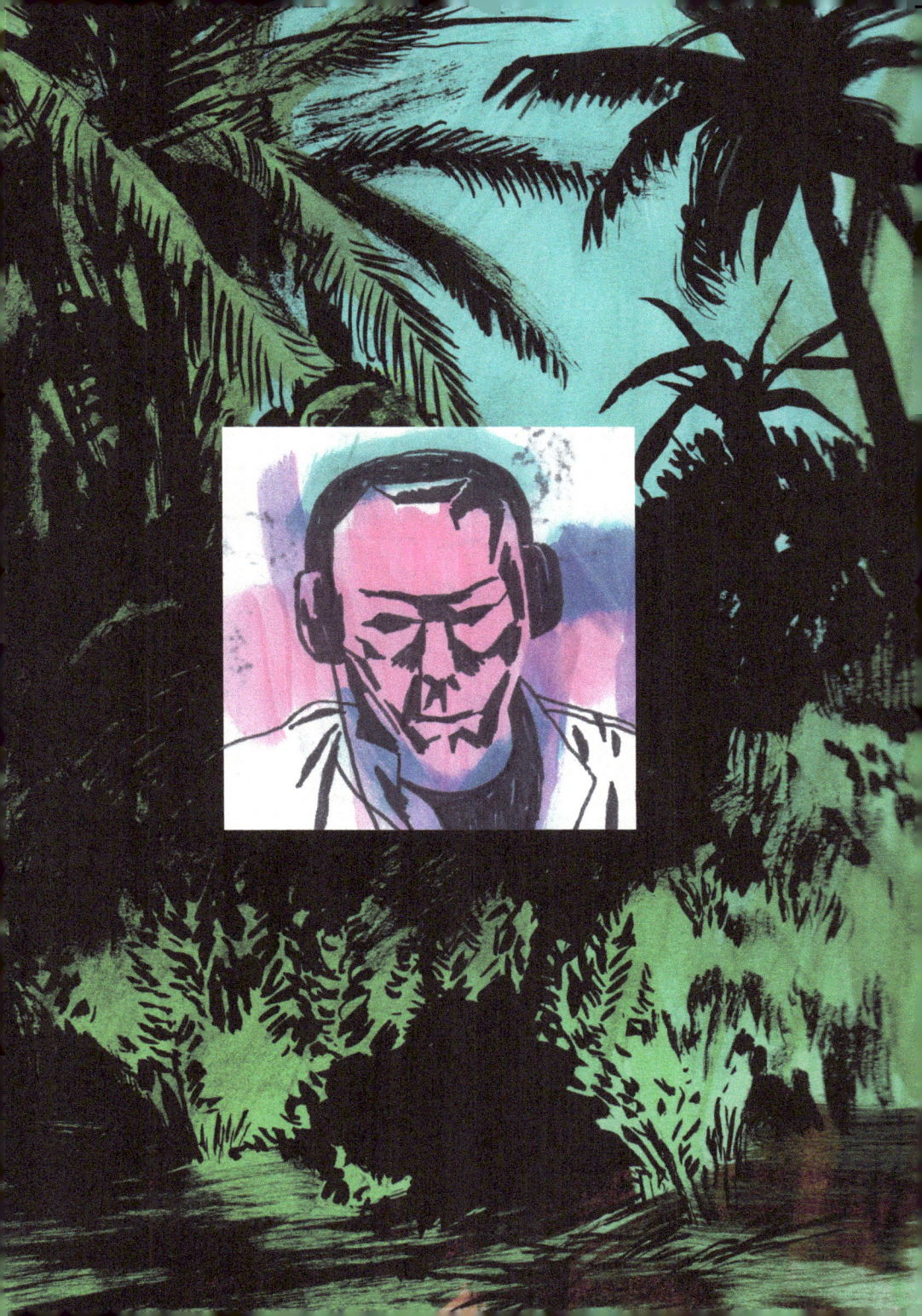

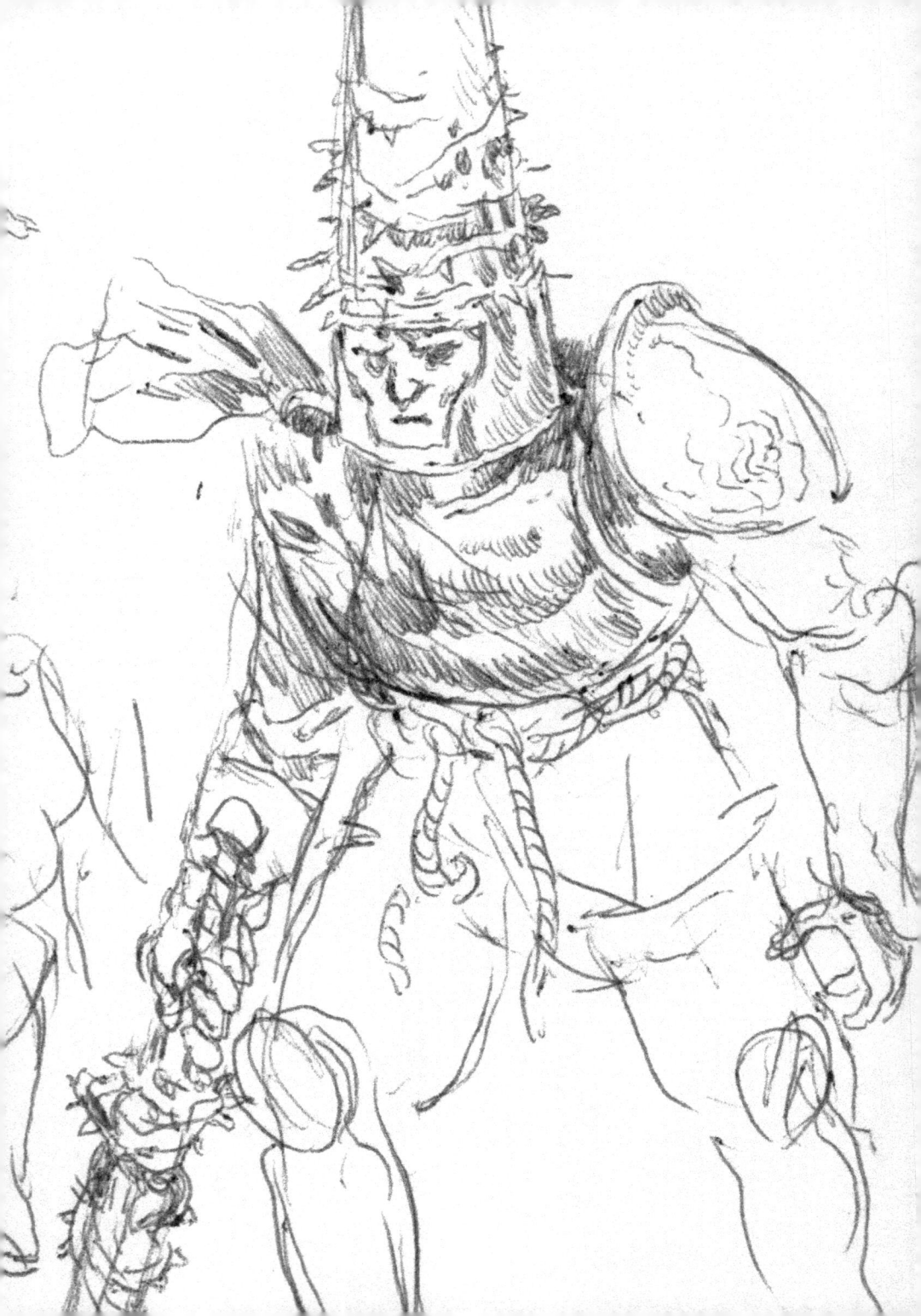

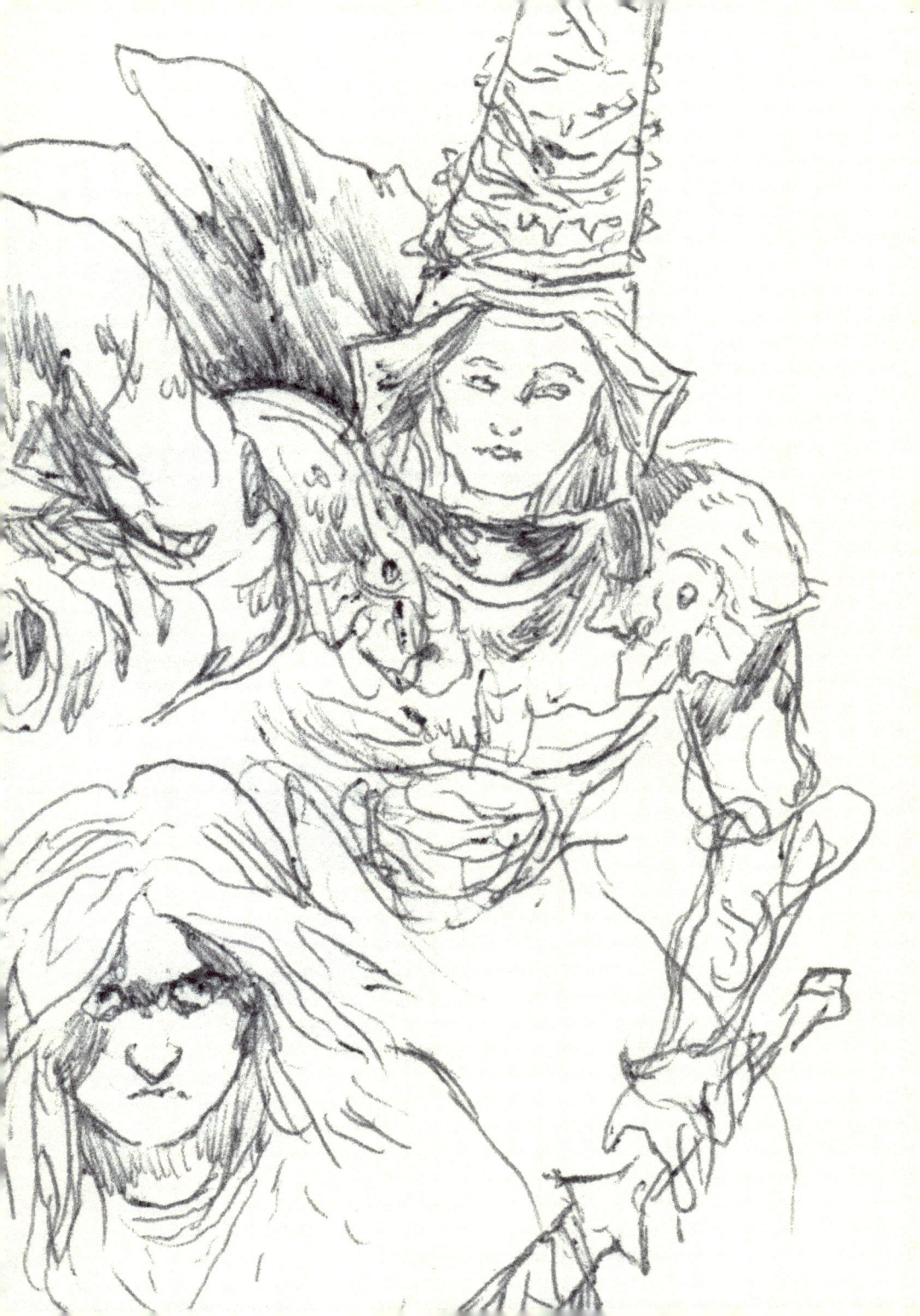

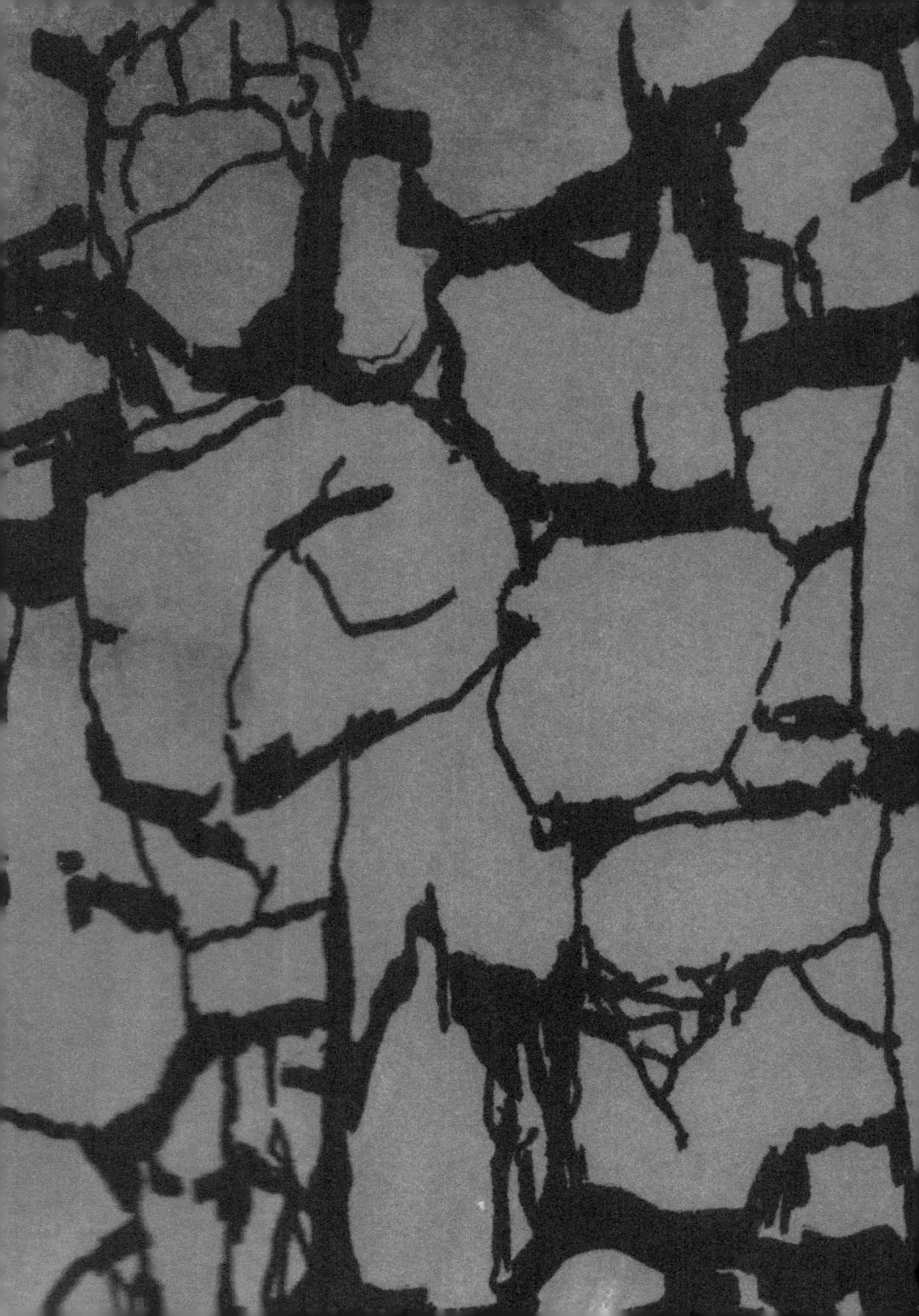

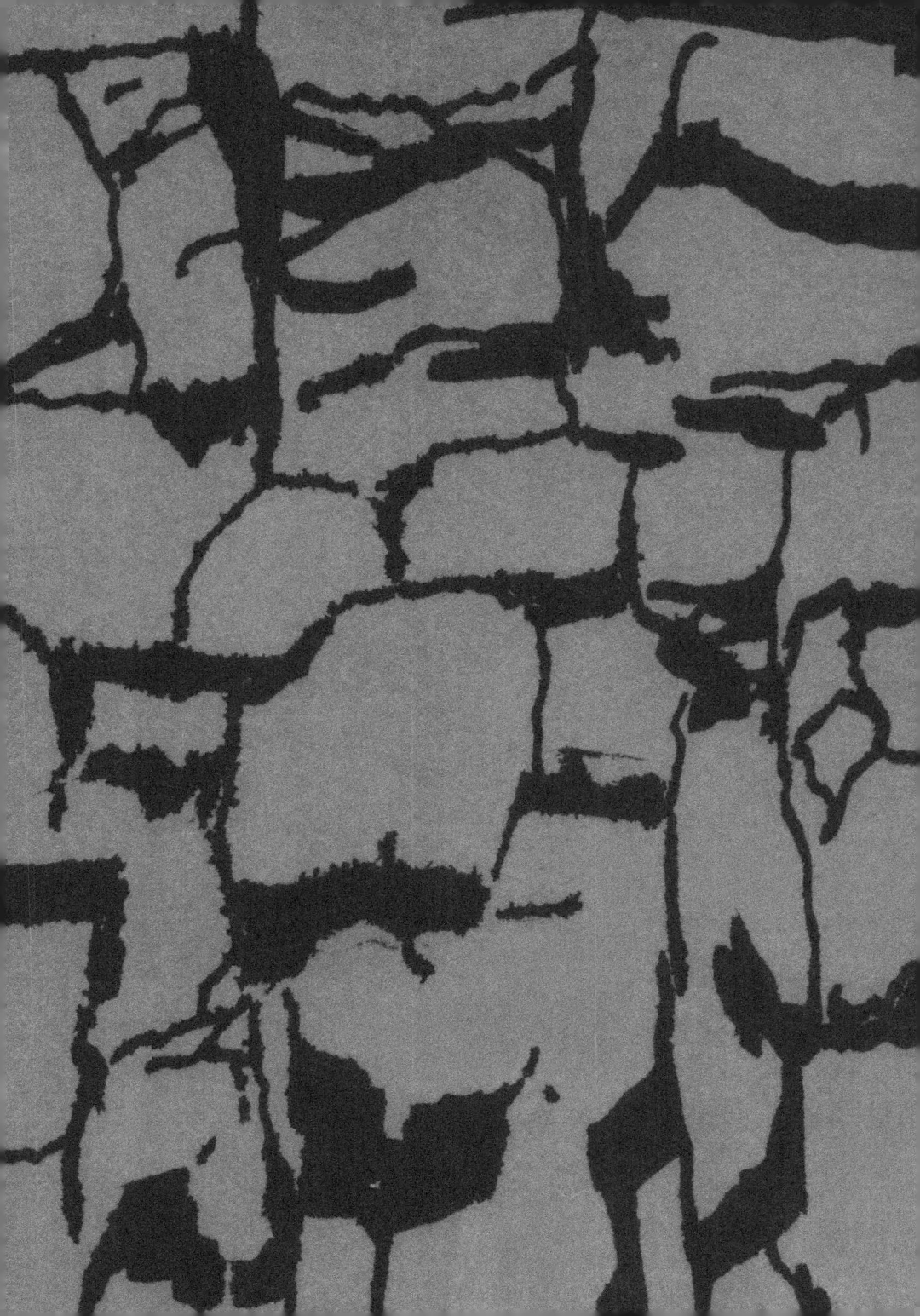

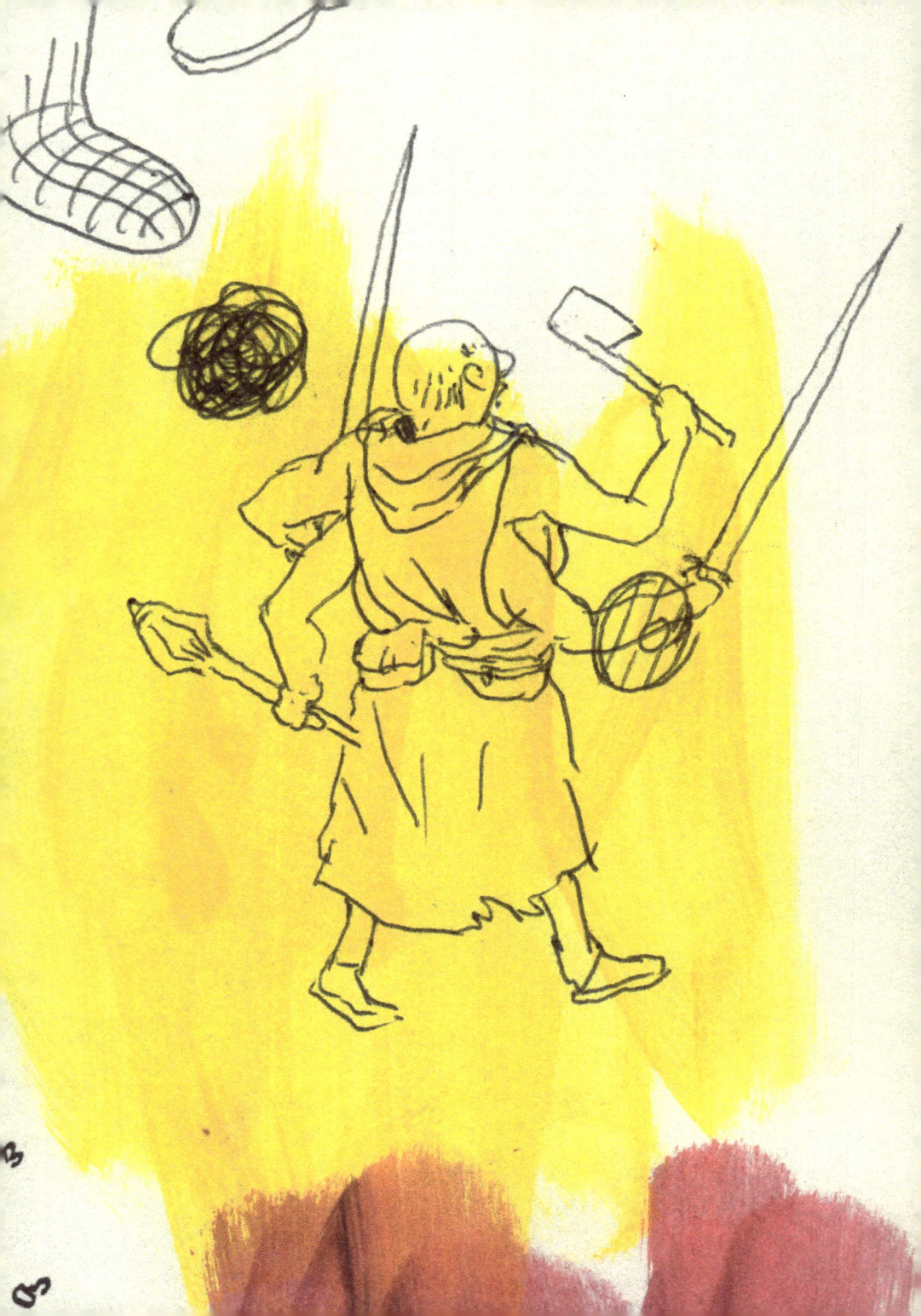

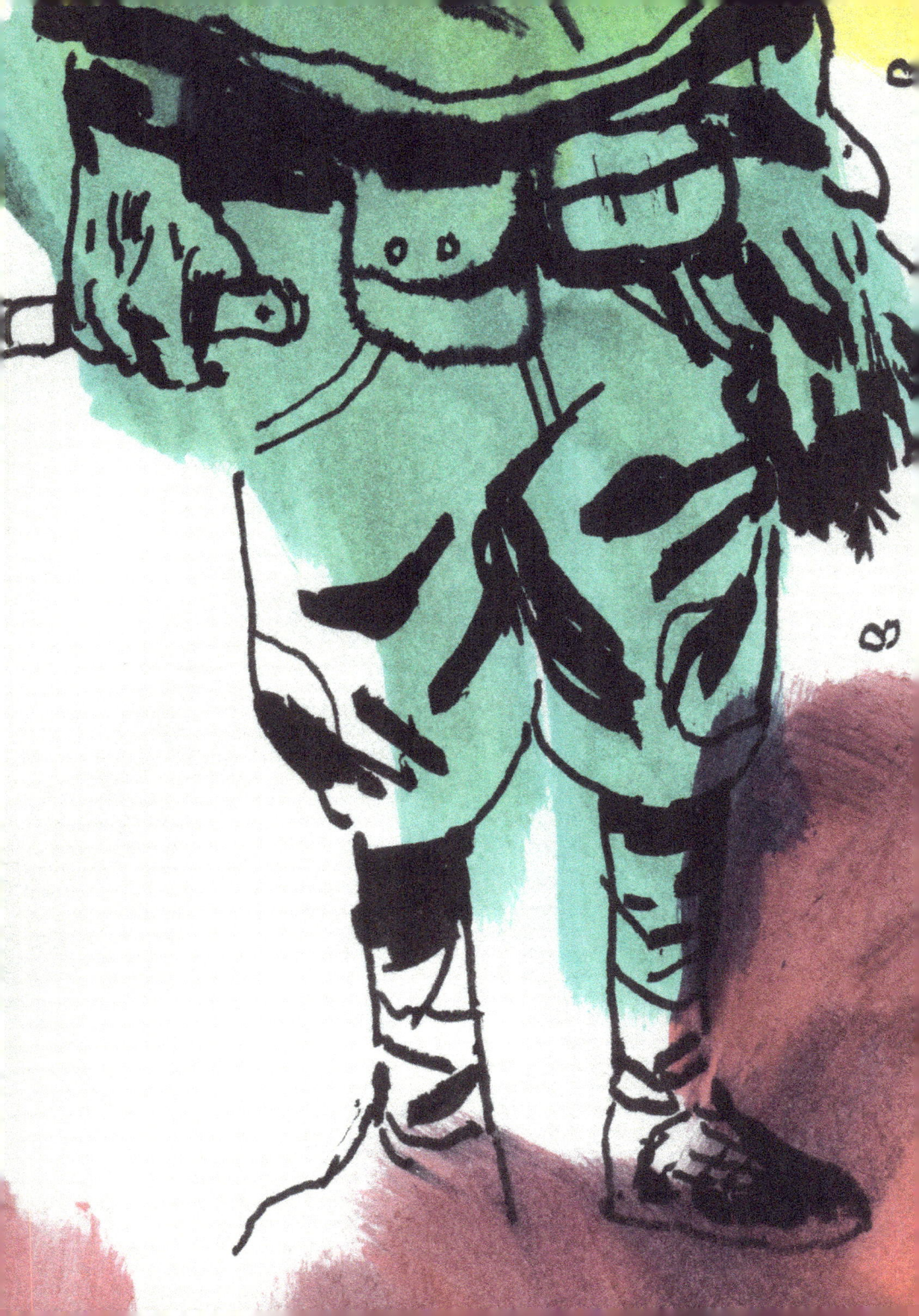

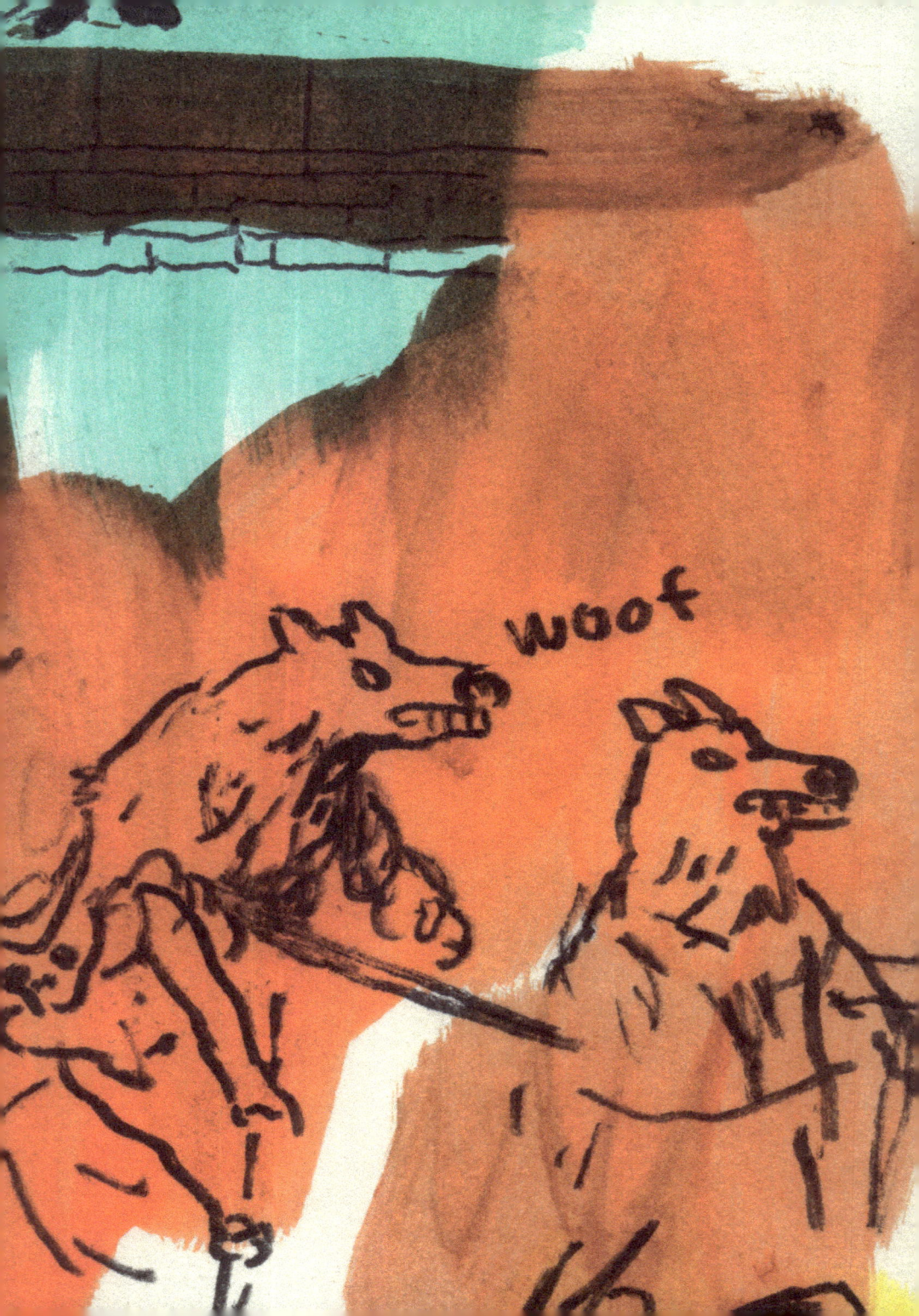

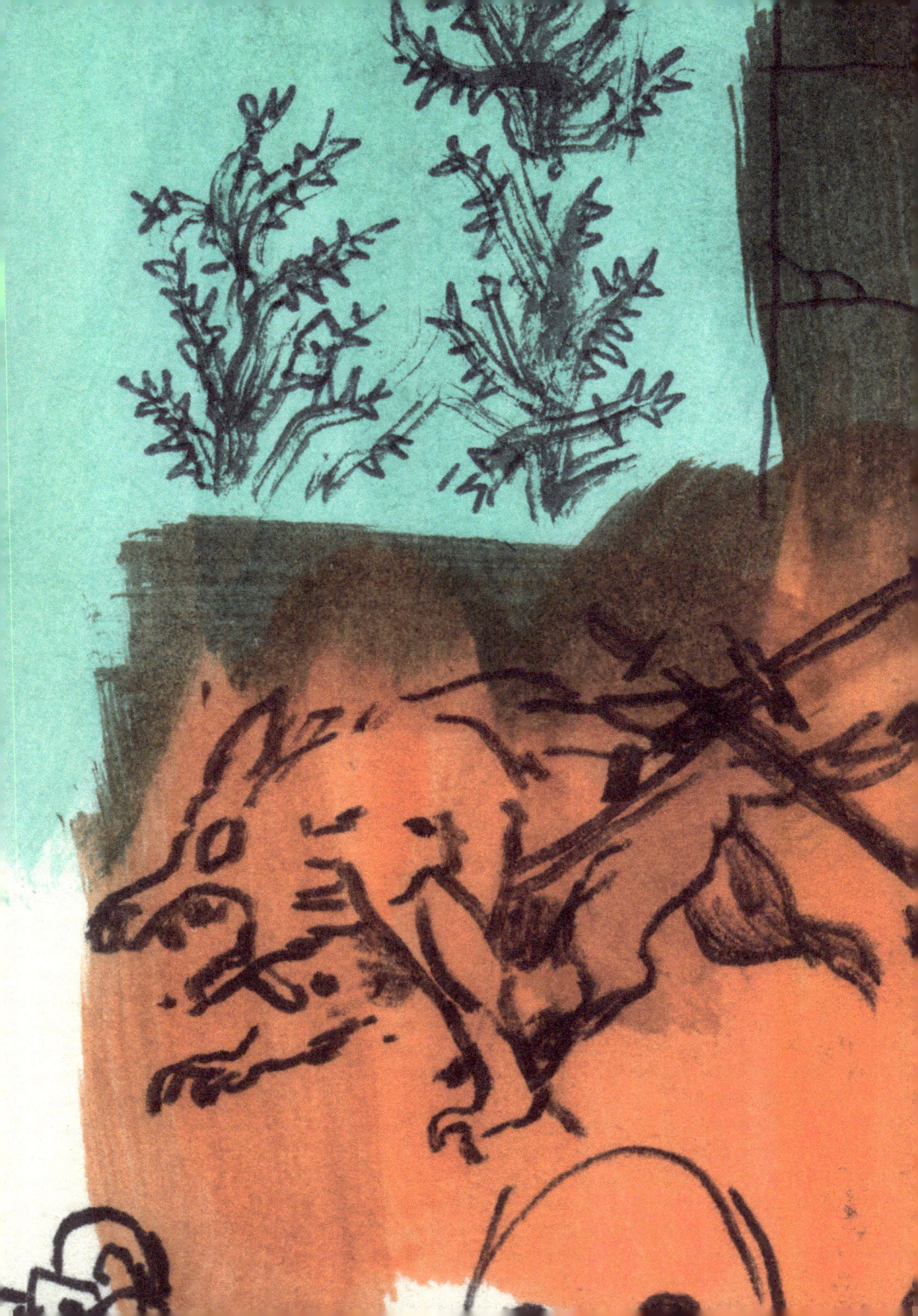

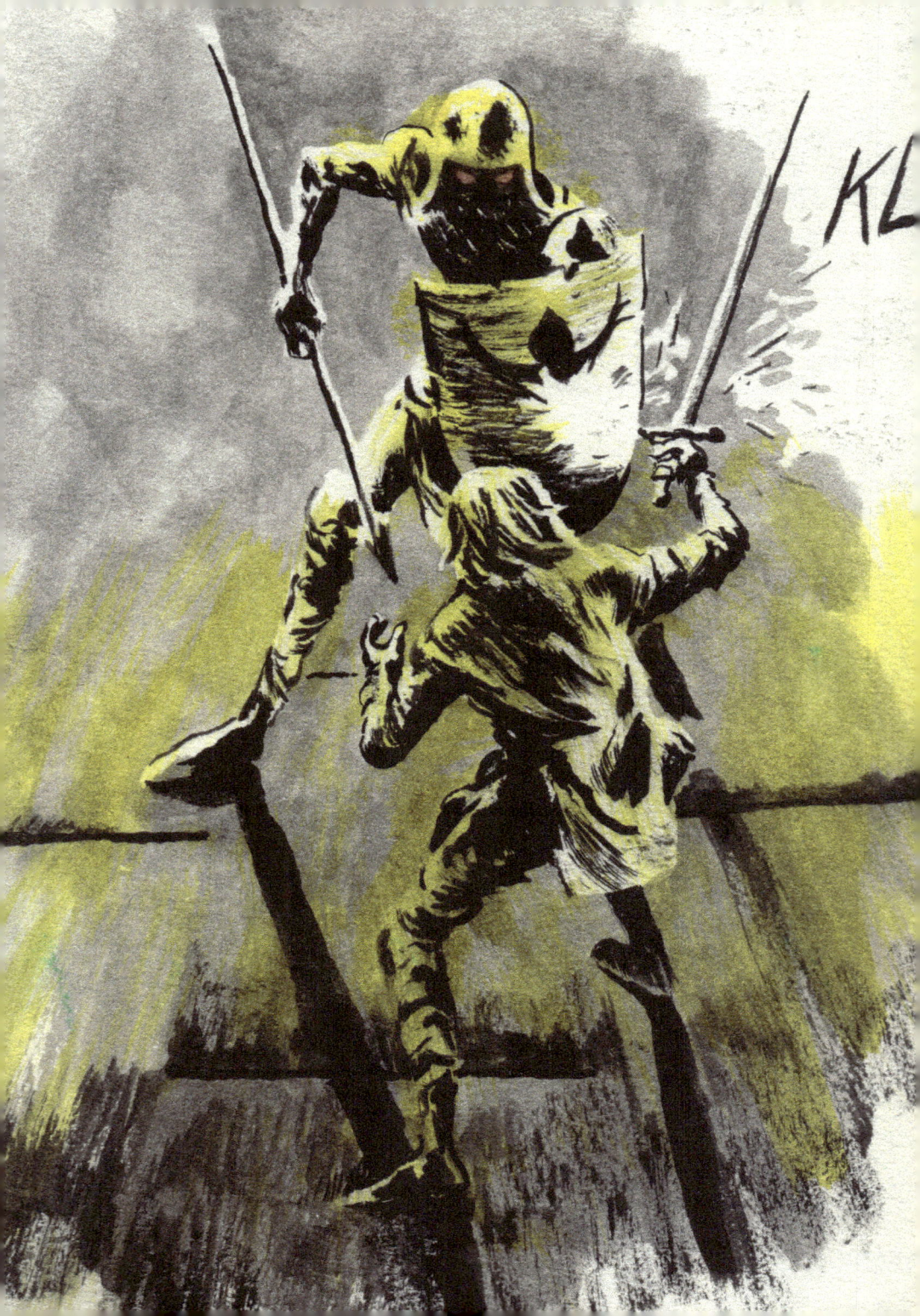

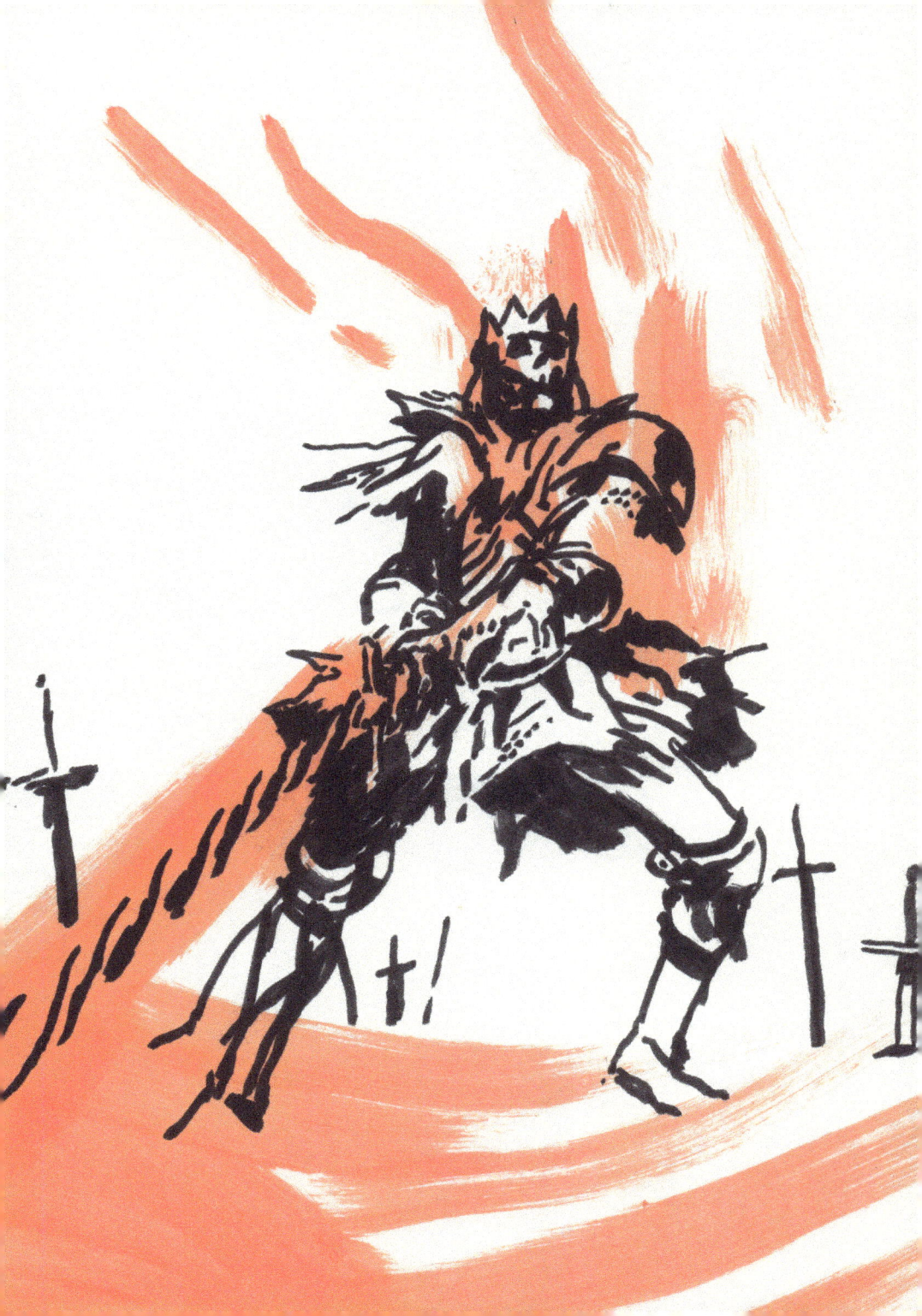

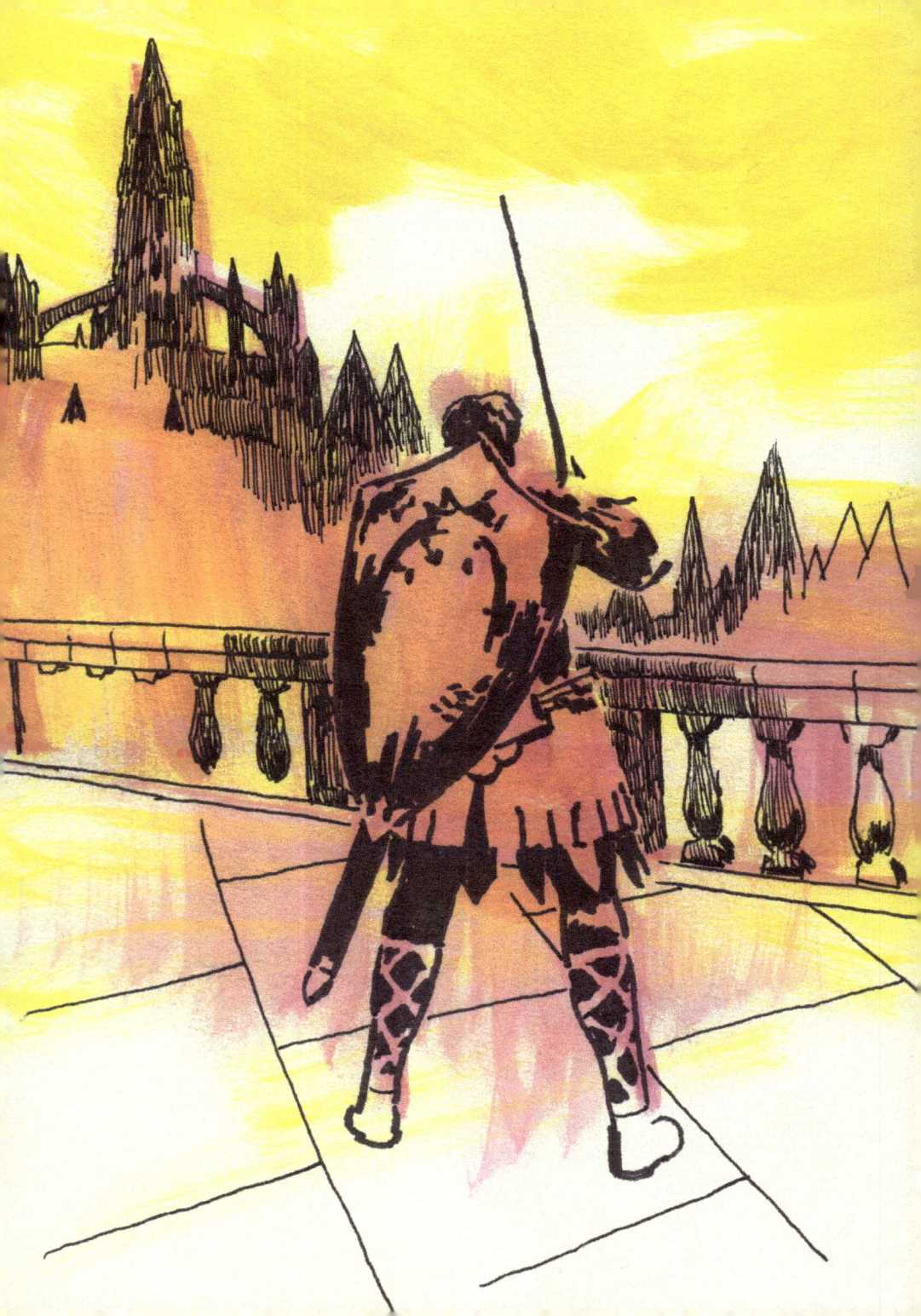